# AAT

INTERMEDIATE



## REVISION **COMPANION** Units 6 & 7

Costing & Reports and Returns

BPP PROFESSIONAL EDUCATION

Fourth edition April 2004
First published 2001

ISBN 07517 1762 2

*British Library Cataloguing-in-Publication Data*
A catalogue record for this book is available from the British Library

Published by

BPP Professional Education
Aldine House,
Aldine Place,
London W12 8AW

Printed in Great Britain by WM Print
Frederick Street
Walsall
West Midlands, WS2 9NE



We are grateful to the AAT for permission to reproduce specimen assessments and simulations and examples from previous assessments. The answers to the specimen simulations for Units 6 and 7 and the specimen exam based assessment for Unit 6 have been published by the AAT. All other answers have been prepared by BPP Professional Education.

# CONTENTS


| | | Questions | Answers |
|---|---|---|---|
| Introduction | | (v) | |
| **Chapter activities** | | | |
| *Unit 6 Recording Cost Information* | | | |
| 1 | Costing information | 1 | 205 |
| 2 | Materials costs | 5 | 209 |
| 3 | Labour costs and expenses | 13 | 218 |
| 4 | Overheads | 15 | 220 |
| 5 | Absorption costing and marginal costing | 19 | 225 |
| 6 | Costing systems | 21 | 229 |
| 7 | Cost bookkeeping | 25 | 233 |
| 8 | Short term decision making | 29 | 237 |
| 9 | Long term decision making | 31 | 239 |
| *Unit 7 Preparing Reports and Returns* | | | |
| 10 | Internal information | 35 | 242 |
| 11 | Performance measures | 37 | 244 |
| 12 | Writing a report | 41 | 248 |
| 13 | Tables and diagrams | 43 | 251 |
| 14 | Reporting figures over time | 47 | 258 |
| 15 | External reporting | 53 | 265 |
| 16 | Value added tax | 59 | 271 |
| 17 | VAT records | 63 | 273 |
| **Practice assessments** | | | |
| *Unit 6* | | | |
| Practice Exam based Assessment 1 – Sports Ltd | | 69 | 277 |
| Practice Exam based Assessment 2 – Plump Ltd | | 81 | 285 |
| Practice Exam based Assessment 3 – Eastley Ltd | | 95 | 295 |
| Practice Exam based Assessment 4 – Gift Ltd | | 109 | 305 |
| AAT Sample Simulation – Quality Candles Ltd | | 119 | 311 |
| *Unit 7* | | | |
| AAT Sample Simulation – Homer Ltd | | 159 | 327 |
| Practice Simulation – Hoddle Ltd | | 181 | 337 |
| Order form | | | |

# INTRODUCTION

This is BPP's innovative AAT Revision Companion for Unit 6, Recording Cost Information and Unit 7, Preparing Reports and Returns. It is part of an integrated package of AAT materials.

It has been written in conjunction with the BPP Course Companion, and has been carefully designed to enable students to practise all aspects of the requirements of the Standards of Competence and performance criteria. It is fully up to date as at April 2004 and reflects the revised Standard of Competence.

This Revision Companion contains these key features:

- graded activities corresponding to each chapter of the Course Companion
- the AAT's sample simulations and answers for Units 6 and 7
- the AAT's sample exam based assessment for Unit 6
- the AAT's exam based assessment for Unit 6 set in December 2003
- two further practice exam based assesments for Unit 6
- a further practice simulation for Unit 7

The emphasis in all activities and questions is on the practical application of the skills acquired.

All activities, practice assessments and simulations have full answers prepared by BPP Professional Education.

A further bank of activities relating to each chapter of the Course Companion and practice assessments, with answers prepared by BPP Professional Education, is available in the Tutor Companion, available only to colleges which adopt the BPP Companion material for these units.

# chapter 1: COSTING INFORMATION

**1** Explain the main differences between financial accounting and cost accounting.

**2** Explain how cost information can be used to assist in the three main roles of management – decision making, planning and control.

**3** Explain how costs are classified in the following ways:

i) capital and revenue costs

ii) according to function

iii) direct and indirect costs

iv) according to behaviour

**4** Show whether each of the following costs would be treated as capital or revenue costs:

| | *Capital* | *Revenue* |
|---|---|---|
| Purchase of a car for resale by a car dealer | | |
| Purchase of a car for use by a salesman | | |
| Road tax payable on purchase of a car for use by a salesman | | |
| Redecorating of head office | | |
| Installing new machinery | | |
| Cleaning of new machinery after initial use | | |

**5** Show how each of the following costs would be classified by function:

| | *Production cost* | *Selling and distribution cost* | *Administration cost* |
|---|---|---|---|
| Depreciation of salesmen's cars | | | |
| Production manager's salary | | | |
| Depreciation of machinery | | | |
| Rent of office space | | | |
| Depreciation of delivery vans | | | |
| Disks for office computer | | | |

**6** Show how each of the following costs would be classified as either a direct cost or an indirect cost:

| | *Direct cost* | *Indirect cost* |
|---|---|---|
| Wages of factory supervisor | | |
| Hire of plant for construction of a building by a building firm | | |
| Cleaning materials used in the factory | | |
| Factory rent | | |
| Wages of a trainee accountant in an accountancy firm | | |
| Cement used for construction of a building by a building firm | | |

**7** Classify each of the following costs according to their behaviour:

i) Telephone bill for line rental and call charges S.V.

ii) Factory rent and rates Fixed.

iii) Materials used in production variable

iv) Supervisor's salary fixed.

v) Warehouse rental where additional space is rented when stock levels are high step fixed

**8** Given below are the output levels and associated production costs for a factory for the last six months:

| | *Output in units* | *Cost* £ |
|---|---|---|
| February | 125,000 | 375,000 |
| March | 142,000 | 418,000 |
| April | 110,000 | 340,000 |
| May | 120,000 | 362,000 |
| June | 145,000 | 424,000 |
| July | 130,000 | 394,000 |

Use the high low method to estimate the variable cost per unit and the overall fixed costs of the factory.

**9** A factory produces a single product which has a raw materials input of £3.80 per unit, labour costs of £1.40 per unit and packaging costs of £0.30 per unit. The factory rent is currently £150,000 per annum but if production levels rise above 120,000 units then additional factory space must be rented at an additional cost of £40,000 per annum. The depreciation of the machinery is £30,000 per annum.

The factory production for the forthcoming year will depend upon the outcome of a promotion of this product and the management hope that production will be for 180,000 units. However if the promotion is not quite as successful as hoped then production will be only 130,000 units. If the promotion is not successful then production will only be for 80,000 units.

Produce a schedule showing the total production costs at each possible level of production.

# chapter 2: MATERIALS COSTS

**1** Complete the following sentences

i) The three main categories of stock for a manufacturing business are ......................................, .......................................... and ..........................................

ii) The internal document used to record the quantity of materials received from a supplier is known as a ................................................

iii) The initial internal document that starts the purchasing process for materials is known as a ................................................

iv) A ........................................................ is the document that is sent to a supplier to request the supply of materials

v) When materials are required from stores by the factory a ............................................ is filled out

vi) A ................................................ is the document received from a supplier of materials requesting payment

**2** Given below is a bin card for one of the materials used by a manufacturing business. During the month of June 2003 the following goods received notes and materials requisitions for this material were completed:

Goods received notes:

| | | |
|---|---|---|
| 3 June | GRN 0326 | 340 units |
| 12 June | GRN 0348 | 300 units |
| 28 June | GRN 0363 | 320 units |

Materials requisitions:

| | | |
|---|---|---|
| 5 June | MR 0295 | 150 units |
| 10 June | MR 0307 | 190 units |
| 20 June | MR 0315 | 180 units |
| 25 June | MR 0320 | 100 units |

Write up the bin card for the month of June 2003.

## BIN CARD

**Description:** 23 Electrical component EC23 **Bin No:** 413

**Code No:**

| Receipts | | | Issues | | | Balance |
|---|---|---|---|---|---|---|
| Date | Reference | Quantity | Date | Reference | Quantity | Quantity |
| 2001 1 June | | | | | | 50 |
| 3 June | GRN0326 | 340 | | | | 390 |
| | | | 5 June | MR0295 | 150 | 240 |
| | | | 10 June | MR0307 | 190 | 50 |
| 12 June | GRN0348 | 300 | | | | 350 |
| | | | 20 June | MR0315 | 180 | 170 |
| | | | 25 June | MR0320 | 100 | 70 |
| 28 June | GRN0363 | 320 | | | | 390 |

**3** Given below are the purchases and issues to production of material XK2 for the month of July 2003:

| | | | |
|---|---|---|---|
| 4 July | Issue | MR 416 | 320 kg |
| 7 July | Purchase | GRN 668 | 500 kg @ £3.20 per kg |
| 12 July | Issue | MR 422 | 180 kg |
| 16 July | Issue | MR 428 | 300 kg |
| 19 July | Purchase | GRN 674 | 500 kg @ £3.50 per kg |
| 23 July | Issue | MR 433 | 230 kg |
| 28 July | Issue | MR 440 | 300 kg |

Opening stock at 1 July consists of 400 kg all purchased at a price of £3.00 per kg.

You are required to write up the stores ledger accounts given below for this material for the month of July 2003 on the following bases:

i) First in first out
ii) Last in first out
iii) Weighted average cost

**STORES LEDGER ACCOUNT**

Stock item XK2

Code 041861

| Date | Receipts | | | | Issues | | | | Balance | |
|---|---|---|---|---|---|---|---|---|---|---|
| | GRN | Qty | Unit price £ | £ | Req No | Qty | Unit price £ | £ | Qty | £ |
| 1 July | | | | | | | | | 400 | 1200.00 |

**STORES LEDGER ACCOUNT**

Stock item XK2

Code 041861

| Date | Receipts | | | | Issues | | | | Balance | |
|---|---|---|---|---|---|---|---|---|---|---|
| | GRN | Qty | Unit price £ | £ | Req No | Qty | Unit price £ | £ | Qty | £ |
| 1 July | | | | | | | | | 400 | 1200.00 |

**STORES LEDGER ACCOUNT**

Stock item XK2

Code 041861

| Date | Receipts | | | | Issues | | | | Balance | |
|---|---|---|---|---|---|---|---|---|---|---|
| | GRN | Qty | Unit price £ | £ | Req No | Qty | Unit price £ | £ | Qty | £ |
| 1 July | | | | | | | | | 400 | 1200.00 |

**4** Given below are the stock movements for component JJ41 for the month of July 2003:

| | | |
|---|---|---|
| 1 July | Opening balance | 220 units @ £5.60 |
| 3 July | Issue | 160 units |
| 7 July | Purchases | 300 units @ £6.00 |
| 10 July | Issue | 170 units |
| 15 July | Issue | 100 units |
| 20 July | Purchases | 250 units @ £6.30 |
| 24 July | Issue | 200 units |

You are required to calculate:

i) the cost of issues
ii) the value of closing stock

in the month of July 2003 using FIFO, LIFO and AVCO methods of stock valuation.

**5** Compare the FIFO and LIFO methods of stock valuation indicating the advantages and disadvantages of each method.

**6** During the month of September 2003 a manufacturing business made purchases of materials on credit totalling £83,469. Stocks of raw materials at 1 September 2003 were valued at £12,523. During September issues of £79,247 were made to the factory for direct production and £6,248 of indirect materials were also issued to the factory.

Write up the cost ledger accounts to reflect these transactions.

**7** Turner & Co sell 40,000 units of one of their stock lines each year. Each unit is purchased on credit at a price of £10 per unit with order costs of £100 per order. The cost of holding one unit of stock for a year is estimated to be 20% of purchase price.

The lead time and the usage per day both tend to vary as follows:

| | *Lead time (days)* | *Usage (units sold per day)* |
|---|---|---|
| Minimum | 2 | 130 |
| Average | 5 | 160 |
| Maximum | 8 | 200 |

a) What is the re-order level?

b) What is the economic order quantity

c) What is the minimum stock level?

d) What is the maximum stock level?

# chapter 3: LABOUR COSTS AND EXPENSES

**1** A business pays its employees on a time rate basis with time and half for any hours worked over 37 hours per week. George is paid a basic rate of £6.80 per hour and during the week ending 31 July 2003 he worked for 43 hours.

Calculate the following figures for the week:

i) George's total gross pay;
ii) the overtime payment;
iii) the overtime premium.

**2** An employee is paid on a differential piecework system on the following basis:

Up to 300 units produced a week – £1.00 per unit

Units over 300 and up to 400 – £1.15 per unit

Any units over 400 – £1.35 per unit

In the week ending 28 June the employee produced 430 units. What is his total gross pay for the week?

**3** A business has a number of different types of employees who are remunerated by different methods. Harry is paid on a piecework basis as follows:

| | |
|---|---|
| Per unit of product A produced | £10.40 |
| Per unit of product B produced | £18.60 |

Stella is paid on a time rate basis at £8.40 per hour for 35 hours a week. For any hours over 35 each week she is paid overtime at the rate of time and a third.

Yvette is paid a salary of £20,000 per annum.

During the week ending 30 June Harry produced 22 units of product A and 7 units of product B and Stella worked for 43 hours. Yvette is paid her salary monthly and for the month of June a performance bonus of 5% of total salary is to be paid to all salaried employees.

Calculate the following figures:

i) Harry's gross pay for the week;
ii) Stella's gross pay for the week;
iii) Yvette's gross pay for the month of June.

**4** The payroll records for a business for the week ending 15 July 2001 show the following details:

| | £ |
|---|---|
| Net pay | 24,700 |
| PAYE and NI deductions | 6,200 |
| Company pension scheme deductions | 2,400 |
| Gross pay | 33,300 |

The payroll analysis also shows that of this total £20,900 relates to direct labour costs and the remainder to indirect labour costs.

Write up the cost ledger accounts to reflect this.

**5** A company owns three classes of fixed assets:

- a freehold building which was purchased for £450,000 including land which was valued at £50,000. Land is not depreciated but the building is depreciated on the basis that it has a remaining useful life of 40 years.
- machinery with an original cost of £220,000. When the machinery was purchased it was estimated that it would have a life of 32,000 hours and would be sold for scrap at the end of this period for £20,000. During the current year the machinery was used for 4,200 hours.
- a fleet of salesman's cars which originally cost £120,000 and which have been depreciated by £52,500 at the start of the year. The cars are depreciated on the reducing balance basis at a rate of 25%.

What is the depreciation charge for each class of fixed assets for the current year?

**6** During the month of October a manufacturing business incurred general production overheads of £39,256. It also paid £7,200 of hire costs in order to replace a machine that had broken down.

Write up the cost ledger accounts to reflect this.

# chapter 4: OVERHEADS

**1** A manufacturing organisation has two production cost centres, the assembly department and the finishing department and two service cost centres, stores and the maintenance department.

The budgeted overheads for the following 6 month period was as follows:

| | *Total* | *Assembly* | *Finishing* | *Stores* | *Maintenance* |
|---|---|---|---|---|---|
| | £ | £ | £ | £ | £ |
| Indirect materials | 18,700 | 16,500 | 2,200 | | |
| Indirect labour | 22,800 | 7,500 | 6,200 | 4,500 | 4,600 |
| Rent and rates | 10,000 | | | | |
| Heat and light | 7,400 | | | | |
| Supervisor's wages | 9,880 | | | | |
| Depreciation of machinery | 8,400 | | | | |

You are also provided with the following information:

| | *Total* | *Assembly* | *Finishing* | *Stores* | *Maintenance* |
|---|---|---|---|---|---|
| Floor area (sq m) | 20,000 | 6,000 | 4,000 | 5,000 | 5,000 |
| Net book value of machinery | £240,000 | £150,000 | £50,000 | £15,000 | £25,000 |
| Supervisor's time in each department (hours) | 38 | 22 | 16 | | |
| Materials requisitions | 300 | 220 | 80 | | |
| Maintenance hours | 1,200 | 700 | 500 | | |

You are to:

i) apportion the overheads to each of the production and service cost centres;

ii) to reapportion the service cost centre costs to the production cost centres (the stores and maintenance cost centres do not provide any services to each other).

**2** A manufacturing organisation has two production departments, A and B, and two service cost centres, stores and the canteen.

The budgeted overheads for the next period are as follows:

| | *Total* | *A* | *B* | *Stores* | *Canteen* |
|---|---|---|---|---|---|
| | £ | £ | £ | £ | £ |
| Indirect wages | 75,700 | 7,800 | 4,700 | 21,200 | 42,000 |
| Rent | 24,000 | | | | |
| Buildings insurance | 2,000 | | | | |
| Power | 6,400 | | | | |
| Heat and light | 4,000 | | | | |
| Supervisor's wages | 10,000 | | | | |
| Machinery depreciation | 3,200 | | | | |
| Machinery insurance | 2,200 | | | | |

You are also provided with the following information:

| | *Total* | *A* | *B* | *Stores* | *Canteen* |
|---|---|---|---|---|---|
| Net book value of machinery | £300,000 | £140,000 | £120,000 | £15,000 | £25,000 |
| Power usage (%) | 100% | 45% | 30% | 5% | 20% |
| Number of employees | 126 | 70 | 40 | 10 | 6 |
| Supervisor's hours | 40 | 25 | 15 | | |
| Floor area (sq m) | 30,000 | 12,000 | 8,000 | 4,000 | 6,000 |
| Materials requisitions | 500 | 300 | 200 | | |

The stores staff use the canteen but the canteen makes no use of the stores services.

You are to:

i) apportion the overheads to each of the production and service cost centres on a fair basis;

ii) reapportion the service cost centre costs to the production cost centres using the step down method.

**3** The overheads for a business have already been apportioned to the two production and two service cost centres that a manufacturing business has as follows:

| Total | Assembly | Polishing | Stores | Maintenance |
|---|---|---|---|---|
| £ | £ | £ | £ | £ |
| 130,000 | 60,000 | 40,000 | 20,000 | 10,000 |

You are also given the following information:

| | *Total* | *Assembly* | *Polishing* | *Stores* | *Maintenance* |
|---|---|---|---|---|---|
| Number of materials requisitions | 400 | 200 | 160 | | 40 |
| Maintenance hours required | 1,000 | 600 | 400 | | |

You are required to reapportion the service cost centre costs using the step down method.

**4** The budgeted overheads of a manufacturing business have been allocated and apportioned to the two production cost centres as follows:

| | |
|---|---|
| Cutting | £58,600 |
| Finishing | £42,400 |

The two production cost centres are budgeted to produce 10,000 units in the next period.

You are also provided with the following further information:

| | *Cutting* | *Finishing* |
|---|---|---|
| Direct labour hours | 4,000 | 24,000 |
| Machine hours | 12,000 | 2,000 |
| Direct labour cost | £24,500 | £168,000 |
| Direct materials cost | £180,000 | £25,000 |
| Prime cost | £204,500 | £193,000 |

You are required to calculate overhead absorption rates on each of the following bases and to state in what circumstances each absorption rate would be appropriate:

i) rate per unit
ii) rate per direct labour hour
iii) rate per machine hour

5 The budgeted overheads apportioned to a business's two production cost centres, C and D, together with the budgeted labour hours and machine hours are given below:

| | C | D |
|---|---|---|
| Overheads | £125,000 | £180,000 |
| Direct labour hours | 12,000 | 80,000 |
| Machine hours | 100,000 | 10,000 |

Production cost centre C is a highly mechanised department with only a few machine operatives whereas production cost centre D is a highly labour intensive department.

i) You are to calculate separate departmental overhead absorption rates for each production cost centre using an appropriate basis and to justify the basis that you have used.

ii) Each unit of Product P spends the following hours in each production department:

| | C | D |
|---|---|---|
| Direct labour hours | 1 | 7 |
| Machine hours | 5 | 2 |

Determine how much overhead will be included in the cost of each unit of product P.

6 In each of the following situations calculate any under or over absorption of overheads and state how they would be dealt with in the profit and loss account:

i) Budgeted production is 1,200 units and budgeted overheads were £5,400. Overheads are to be absorbed on a unit basis. The actual production was 1,000 units and the overheads incurred were £5,000.

ii) Budgeted production was 600 units to be produced in 1,800 labour hours. Budgeted overheads of £5,040 are to be absorbed on a direct labour hour basis. The actual production for the period was 700 units in 2,200 labour hours and the actual overheads were £5,100.

iii) Budgeted production was 40,000 units and the budgeted machine hours per unit was 2 hours per unit. Budgeted overheads were £320,000 and were to be absorbed on a machine hour basis. The actual overheads incurred were £320,000 and the production was 42,000 units. The total machine hours were 82,000.

7 Using the data from the previous activity write up the production overhead control account in each case clearly showing the transfer to the profit and loss account for under/over absorption of overheads.

# chapter 5: ABSORPTION COSTING AND MARGINAL COSTING

1 A business produces a single product in its factory which has two production departments, cutting and finishing. In the following quarter it is anticipated that 120,000 units of the product will be produced. The expected costs are:

| | | |
|---|---|---|
| Direct materials | | £12 per unit |
| Direct labour | | 2 hours cutting @ £7.40 per hour |
| | | 1 hour finishing @ £6.80 per hour |
| Variable overheads | cutting | £336,000 |
| | finishing | £132,000 |
| Fixed overheads | cutting | £144,000 |
| | finishing | £96,000 |

Overheads are absorbed on the basis of direct labour hours.

What is the unit cost under absorption costing and under marginal costing?

2 Given below are the budgeted production and sales figures for the single product that a business makes and sells for the months of July and August.

| | July | August |
|---|---|---|
| Production | 24,000 units | 24,000 units |
| Sales | 22,000 units | 25,000 units |

There were stocks of 1,500 units of the product at the start of July.

The expected production costs for each of the two months are:

| | |
|---|---|
| Direct materials | £6.80 per unit |
| Direct labour | £3.60 per unit |
| Variable production costs | £32,400 |
| Fixed production costs | £44,400 |

Overheads are absorbed on the basis of the budgeted production level and the product is sold for £16 per unit.

a) Prepare the budgeted profit and loss account for the two months using:

i) absorption costing
ii) marginal costing

b) Prepare a reconciliation explaining any difference in the two profit figures in each of the two months.

**3** You are given the budgeted data about the production of a business's single product for the following quarter:

| | |
|---|---|
| Opening stock | 840 units |
| Production | 8,000 units |
| Sales | 8,200 units |
| Direct materials | £23.60 |
| Direct labour | 4 hours @ £5.80 per hour |
| Variable overheads | £88,000 |
| Fixed overheads | £51,200 |

Overheads are absorbed on the basis of units of production The product has a selling price of £70 per unit.

a) Prepare the budgeted profit and loss account for the quarter using:

i) absorption costing
ii) marginal costing

b) Prepare a reconciliation explaining any difference in the profit using absorption costing and profit using marginal costing.

**4** Explain why marginal costing may be a more appropriate method than absorption costing for costing and reporting purposes.

# chapter 6: COSTING SYSTEMS

1 Explain when the use of job costing is appropriate.

2 A manufacturer of custom made bedroom furniture has been asked to supply bedroom fittings for a customer. The estimated costs are given below:

Materials for units – £2,800
Direct labour for fitting units – 27 hours @ £19.50 per hour
Overheads are absorbed on the basis of £8.70 per direct labour hour
Profit on each job is 20% of total costs
VAT is charged at 17.5%

You are to prepare a job costing schedule showing how much the bedroom fittings will cost the customer.

**3** Given below is a job costing schedule based on the estimates made which is still to be completed.

**JOB NUMBER 2856**

| | £<br>*Budget* | £<br>*Actual* | £<br>*Variance* |
|---|---|---|---|
| Direct materials | | | |
| ■ wood | 1,650.00 | | |
| ■ components | 830.00 | | |
| ■ plastic | 320.00 | | |
| Direct labour | | | |
| ■ Grade I – 30hours | 414.00 | | |
| ■ Grade III – 12 hours | 132.00 | | |
| Direct expenses | | | |
| ■ hire of equipment | 300.00 | | |
| Overheads | | | |
| Total cost | | | |
| Profit | | | |
| VAT | | | |

Overheads are absorbed into the cost of jobs at a rate of £4.60 per direct labour hour. Profit on jobs is 25% of total cost and VAT is charged at a rate of 17.5%.

On the completion of the job the cost of the wood was £1,830.00, the components £755.00 and the plastic £300. In total 33 hours of Grade I labour were charged to the job at a rate of £14.50 per hour and 7 hours of Grade III labour were charged at an hourly rate of £11.00. The equipment hired had to be kept for an additional two days increasing the hire cost to £380.

You are required to:

i) complete the costing of the job to show the price to be charged to the customer;

ii) compare the actual costs to the budgeted costs showing the variances;

iii) complete the job costing schedule at the end of the job showing the final profit that was actually earned on the job.

**4** Given below are the details for a process for the month of May:

| | | |
|---|---|---|
| Direct materials | 100,000 kg | £287,000 |
| Direct labour | | £138,000 |
| Overheads | | £82,600 |
| Normal loss | | 6% |
| Output | | 92,000 kg |

Write up the ledger accounts to record the process results for the month.

**5** Given below are the details for a process for the first week in March:

| | | |
|---|---|---|
| Direct materials | 18,000 litres | £35,800 |
| Direct labour | | £ 7,200 |
| Overheads | | £11,720 |

The normal loss from the process is 5% and the output for the week was 17,500 litres.

Write up the ledger accounts to reflect the process costs for the week.

**6** Given below are the details of a process for the month of March. Any loss units can be sold for scrap for £2.00 per kg.

| | | |
|---|---|---|
| Direct materials | 50,000 kgs | £356,400 |
| Direct labour | | £120,500 |
| Overheads | | £41,600 |
| Normal loss | | 10% |
| Output | | 42,000 kg |

Write up the ledger accounts to reflect the process results for the month.

# chapter 7: COST BOOKKEEPING

1 A manufacturing business absorbs production overheads into work in progress at a rate of £3.20 per direct labour hour. In the month of August 2003 the overheads incurred totalled £4,720 and the direct labour hours worked were 1,400.

Write up the production overhead control account. Explain the accounting treatment of any balance on the account.

2 A manufacturing business absorbs production overheads at a rate of £6.45 per direct labour hour. In the month of July 2003 a total of 940 direct labour hours were worked and the production overhead incurred was £5,840.

Write up the production overhead control account and explain the accounting treatment of any balance on the account.

3 A manufacturing business has the following transactions for the week ending 7 September 2003:

| | | |
|---|---|---|
| Materials purchased on credit | | £14,365 |
| Materials requisitions from the factory | | £11,632 |
| Total payroll costs | – direct factory labour | £18,375 |
| | – indirect factory labour | £2,682 |
| Production overheads incurred | | £6,243 |
| Production overheads to be absorbed | | 1,530 hours @ £5.20 per hour |
| Transfer of production to finished goods | | £36,540 |

Write up the following ledger accounts in an integrated cost bookkeeping system to reflect these transactions:

- Materials control account
- Wages control account
- Production overhead control account
- Work in progress control account

**4** Given below are extracts from the trial balance of a business at 1 August 2003:

| | *Debit* | *Credit* |
|---|---|---|
| | £ | £ |
| Stock: | | |
| Raw materials | 1,290 | |
| Work in Progress | 1,540 | |
| Finished goods | 1,830 | |
| Debtors | 7,200 | |
| Creditors | | 5,460 |
| Cash at bank | 3,070 | |

You are also given a summary of some of the transactions of the business for the month of August:

| | | £ |
|---|---|---|
| Materials purchased on credit | | 7,640 |
| Materials requisitions | – factory | 6,620 |
| | – administration | 990 |
| Wages cost | – direct factory labour (490 hours) | 5,430 |
| | – indirect factory labour | 1,460 |
| Sales invoices issued | | 14,700 |
| Cheques received from debtors | | 6,800 |
| Cheques paid to creditors | | 4,900 |
| Production transferred to finished goods | | 12,200 |
| Production overheads paid by cheque | | 4,290 |
| Administration overheads paid by cheque | | 1,210 |
| Closing stock of finished goods | | 1,650 |

Production overheads are absorbed at the budgeted overhead absorption rate of £11.10 per direct labour hour.

You are required to:

i) write up the ledger accounts given below to reflect these transactions and to balance each of the accounts at the end of the month;

ii) prepare the profit and loss account for the month.

Materials control account

| | £ | | £ |
|---|---|---|---|
| | | | |

Wages control account

| | £ | | £ |
|---|---|---|---|
| | | | |

Production overhead control account

| | £ | | £ |
|---|---|---|---|
| | | | |

Work in progress control account

| | £ | | £ |
|---|---|---|---|
| | | | |

Finished goods control account

| | £ | | £ |
|---|---|---|---|
| | | | |

Debtors control account

| | £ | | £ |
|---|---|---|---|
| | | | |

Creditors control account

| | £ | | £ |
|---|---|---|---|
| | | | |

Cash at bank account

| | £ | | £ |
|---|---|---|---|
| | | | |

Administration overheads account

| | £ | | £ |
|---|---|---|---|
| | | | |

Sales account

| | £ | | £ |
|---|---|---|---|
| | | | |

# chapter 8: SHORT TERM DECISION MAKING

1 When making decisions about production and sales in the short term explain why contribution per unit is a more useful figure than total production cost per unit.

2 A business sells a single product and has budgeted sales of 115,000 units for the next period. The selling price per unit is £28 and the variable costs of production are £17. The fixed costs of the business are £1,100,000.

What is the break-even point in units and the margin of safety?

3 A business sells a single product at a selling price of £83 and the variable costs of production and sales are £65 per unit. The fixed costs of the business are £540,000.

How many units of the product must the business sell in order to make a profit of £300,000?

4 A business sells its single product for £40. The variable costs of this product total £28. The fixed costs of the business are £518,000.

What is the sales revenue required in order to make a profit of £250,000.

**5** A business produces three products. Production and sales details are given below:

| | *Product* | | |
|---|---|---|---|
| | *R* | *S* | *T* |
| Direct materials @ £5 per kg | £20 | £25 | £15 |
| Direct labour @ £7 per hour | £14 | £21 | £21 |
| Selling price | £45 | £60 | £55 |
| Machine hours per unit | 4 | 3 | 2 |
| Maximum sales demand | 20,000 units | 25,000 units | 8,000 units |

During the next period the supply of materials is limited to 250,000 kgs, the labour hours available are 100,000 and the machine hours available are 180,000.

What is the production plan which will maximise contribution and what is the contribution that will be earned under that production plan?

# chapter 9:
# LONG TERM DECISION MAKING

1 Explain what is meant by the time value of money.

2 Given below are the anticipated cash flows from investment in new plant and machinery that a business is considering.

| | | £ |
|---|---|---|
| 1 Jan 2003 | Outflow | 95,000 |
| 31 Dec 2003 | Inflow | 15,000 |
| 31 Dec 2004 | Inflow | 25,000 |
| 31 Dec 2005 | Inflow | 35,000 |
| 31 Dec 2006 | Inflow | 30,000 |
| 31 Dec 2007 | Inflow | 30,000 |

a) The business policy is only to accept projects with a payback period of 3 years or less. On this basis would you advise the managers of the business to invest in this project?

b) The business has a cost of capital of 10%. Calculate the net present value of the project. Would you now change your advice to the managers of the business?

c) State any assumptions that you have made in parts (a) and (b).

d) What might this situation indicate about the payback period method of investment appraisal?

3 Today's date is 1 April 2003. What is the present value of each of the following independent cash flows?

i) Payment of £24,000 on 31 March 2005 – interest rate 7%
ii) Receipt of £1,500 on 31 March 2004, 2005 and 2006 – interest rate 12%
iii) Receipt of £2,000 every 31 March from 2004 onwards – interest rate 6%
iv) Payment of £30,000 on 1 April 2003 – interest rate 8%
v) Receipt of £700 on 1 April 2003 and every 31 March until 2007 – interest rate 5%

**4** A company is considering the purchase of a small sole trader's business for a cost of £84,000 on 30 June 2003. The estimated cash inflows from the purchased business are:

| | £ |
|---|---|
| 30 June 2004 | 26,000 |
| 30 June 2005 | 30,000 |
| 30 June 2006 | 21,000 |
| 30 June 2007 | 14,000 |

Thereafter the purchased business will be closed down and its operations merged with the other operations of the company.

The company has a cost of capital of 7% and analyses potential investments using the net present value method.

What would your advice be to the directors of the company concerning the purchase of the sole trader's business? Justify that advice.

**5** The managers of a business are considering investing in a new factory. It has been estimated that the cost now would total £355,000. The anticipated profit for the factory for each of the next 5 years are as follows:

| | *Profit* £ |
|---|---|
| Year 1 | 47,000 |
| Year 2 | 55,000 |
| Year 3 | 68,000 |
| Year 4 | 53,000 |
| Year 5 | 22,000 |

The profit figures given are after charging depreciation of £60,000 in each year. The business has a cost of capital of 12%.

a) What is the net present value of the potential investment?
b) State any assumptions that you have made in your calculations.
c) What would be your advice to the managers about this potential investment?

**6** The managers of a business are considering investment in a new production line which would cost £180,000 on 1 October 2003. The estimated cash cost savings from the new production line are:

| | £ |
|---|---|
| 30 Sept 2004 | 42,000 |
| 30 Sept 2005 | 50,000 |
| 30 Sept 2006 | 75,000 |
| 30 Sept 2007 | 80,000 |

By the end of September 2007 the production line will require replacing.

a) Calculate the NPV of the project at the company's cost of capital of 15%, and state whether the company should accept the project. Justify your conclusion.

b) The company may be able to obtain finance for the project with an interest rate of 10%. Re-evaluate whether the project is worthwhile at this new cost of capital.

c) The internal rate of return (IRR) of the project is 12.5%. Explain the meaning of the IRR and why this can be useful in project evaluation.

# chapter 10: INTERNAL INFORMATION

1 Knight Industrial makes a range of electronic components in its factory. The factory employees clock in and out using clock cards and work a standard 35 hour week. Any hours that are worked in excess of the 35 hours are paid at time and a half if on a week day and double time at weekends.

What type of information about the labour force would be likely to be required by the following personnel in the organisation?

i) the factory supervisor
ii) the manufacturing director
iii) the managing director

2 Outline what are the general requirements of useful information.

3 What would be the typical type of information that might be required by the partners in a firm of solicitors in order to appraise the performance of the firm for the last month?

4 Kenzo Stores has three shops in Abberville, Bacup and Calver. Given below are the summarised profit and loss accounts for the three stores for the month of July 2003.

| | Abberville | Bacup | Calver |
|---|---|---|---|
| | £ | £ | £ |
| Sales | 137,489 | 195,374 | 104,328 |
| Cost of sales | 53,621 | 72,288 | 41,731 |
| Gross profit | 83,868 | 123,086 | 62,597 |
| Expenses | 33,373 | 37,121 | 22,952 |
| Net profit | 50,495 | 85,965 | 39,645 |

You are required to produce the consolidated profit and loss account figures for the three stores for the month of July 2003.

# chapter 11: PERFORMANCE MEASURES

1 A manufacturing business has produced 330,000 of its product in the quarter ending 30 June 2003 at a total manufacturing cost of £567,900. The budgeted production for the quarter had been 350,000 units and the actual hours worked in the quarter were 12,600.

In the quarter ending 31 March 2003 the budgeted production was 320,000 units and actual production was 332,000 units. This production level was achieved in 12,300 hours and the total cost of production in that quarter was £580,400.

Calculate the following performance measures for the quarter ending 30 June 2003 and compare them to the same performance measures for the previous quarter:

- cost per unit
- labour productivity
- productivity index

2 A mail order manufacturing business employs 280 factory employees and 27 telephone sales staff. For the month of July 2003 the following performance figures were available:

| | |
|---|---|
| Units produced | 128,700 |
| Budgeted units | 120,000 |
| Manufacturing cost of units produced | £557,800 |
| Factory labour hours | 39,400 |
| Telephone orders processed | 9,180 |
| Telephone sales department costs | £14,560 |

From the information given produce a schedule that summarises the performance of the factory and the telephone sales department for the month.

3 Explain the difference between avoidable and unavoidable idle time.

**4** The number of labour hours worked and the number of idle time hours for a factory for the last six months was as follows:

| | *Jan* | *Feb* | *Mar* | *Apr* | *May* | *June* |
|---|---|---|---|---|---|---|
| Hours worked | 2,100 | 2,050 | 2,220 | 2,200 | 2,310 | 2,250 |
| Idle time hours | 90 | 80 | 20 | 100 | 120 | 100 |

The hours worked plus the idle time hours total to the number of hours available for work in the month.

Calculate the labour utilisation percentage for each of the six months to one decimal place.

**5** You are given the following information about a business for the last three months:

| | *May* | *June* | *July* |
|---|---|---|---|
| Sales | £360,000 | £402,000 | £398,000 |
| Capital | £300,000 | £310,000 | £320,000 |
| NBV of fixed assets | £210,000 | £190,000 | £200,000 |
| Machine hours worked | 28,000 | 32,000 | 31,000 |

For each of the three months calculate measures to indicate the fixed asset utilisation, machinery utilisation and capital utilisation or asset turnover.

**6** Given below are the summarised profit and loss accounts for a business for the last three months:

| | *May* | *June* | *July* |
|---|---|---|---|
| | £'000 | £'000 | £'000 |
| Sales | 1,320 | 1,420 | 1,500 |
| Cost of sales | 790 | 850 | 970 |
| | 530 | 570 | 530 |
| Expenses | 290 | 330 | 290 |
| Net profit | 240 | 240 | 240 |

The capital of the business was as follows for the three months:

| | *May* | *June* | *July* |
|---|---|---|---|
| | £'000 | £'000 | £'000 |
| Capital | 2,600 | 2,840 | 3,080 |

Prepare a schedule showing the gross profit margin, net profit margin and return on capital employed for each of the three months, calculated to one decimal place, making brief comment as to what the performance measures indicate about the business.

7 Given below is a variety of information about a manufacturing business for the last three months:

| | *May* | *June* | *July* |
|---|---|---|---|
| Sales | £595,000 | £600,000 | £610,000 |
| Manufacturing cost | £416,000 | £402,000 | £403,000 |
| Expenses | £131,000 | £144,000 | £149,000 |
| Number of units produced | 220,000 | 215,000 | 216,000 |
| Budgeted number of units | 220,000 | 220,000 | 220,000 |
| Hours worked | 1,400 | 1,360 | 1,430 |
| Budgeted hours | 1,400 | 1,400 | 1,400 |
| Net book value of fixed assets | £320,000 | £300,000 | £340,000 |
| Capital | £460,000 | £508,000 | £562,000 |

You are required to calculate the following performance measures and to comment on the results that you find:

i) Cost per unit
ii) Productivity per labour hour
iii) Productivity index
iv) Labour utilisation percentage
v) Fixed asset utilisation
vi) Asset turnover (capital utilisation)
vii) Gross profit margin
viii) Net profit margin
ix) Return on capital employed

# chapter 12: WRITING A REPORT

**1** What are the major elements of a report?

**2** Given below are the summarised profit and loss account figures for one shop that is part of a chain of retail stores for the last six months.

| | *Jan* | *Feb* | *Mar* | *Apr* | *May* | *June* |
|---|---|---|---|---|---|---|
| | £'000 | £'000 | £'000 | £'000 | £'000 | £'000 |
| Sales | 420 | 450 | 500 | 550 | 580 | 630 |
| Cost of sales | 248 | 261 | 285 | 310 | 325 | 345 |
| Gross profit | 172 | 189 | 215 | 240 | 255 | 285 |
| Expenses | 110 | 119 | 145 | 160 | 165 | 190 |
| Net profit | 62 | 70 | 70 | 80 | 90 | 95 |
| Capital | 660 | 720 | 780 | 810 | 840 | 900 |

Write a report on the profitability of the shop for the last six months for the sales director showing any performance indicators that can be calculated in an appendix.

Today's date is 19 August 2003.

**3** Given below are productivity details of the three manufacturing divisions of an organisation, which each produce the same product, for the last quarter.

| | *Division A* | *Division B* | *Division C* |
|---|---|---|---|
| Number of units produced | 400,000 | 240,000 | 300,000 |
| Cost of manufacture | £1,248,000 | £739,200 | £915,000 |
| Hours worked | 14,000 | 8,000 | 10,400 |
| Budgeted production – units | 450,000 | 250,000 | 330,000 |
| Budgeted hours | 15,000 | 8,333 | 11,000 |

You are required to write a report commenting to the manufacturing director upon the productivity of the three divisions.

Today's date is 20 July 2003.

# chapter 13: TABLES AND DIAGRAMS

1 You are given the following information about a company for the last four months.

| | *June* | *July* | *Aug* | *Sept* |
|---|---|---|---|---|
| | £ | £ | £ | £ |
| Sales | 48,700 | 50,200 | 45,600 | 46,800 |
| Cost of sales | 30,200 | 31,600 | 29,200 | 30,000 |
| Expenses | 12,200 | 12,500 | 11,400 | 11,700 |
| Capital | 52,500 | 52,500 | 55,000 | 55,000 |

a) Prepare a computer spreadsheet which will calculate the following performance measures by inserting appropriate formulae:

i) gross profit percentage
ii) net profit percentage
iii) return on capital employed
iv) asset turnover

| | A | B | C | D | E |
|---|---|---|---|---|---|
| 1 | | | | | |
| 2 | | | | | |
| 3 | | | | | |
| 4 | | | | | |
| 5 | | | | | |
| 6 | | | | | |
| 7 | | | | | |
| 8 | | | | | |
| 9 | | | | | |
| 10 | | | | | |
| 11 | | | | | |

b) Show the figures for these performance measures that would appear once the computer package has been run.

| | A | B | C | D | E |
|---|---|---|---|---|---|
| 1 | | | | | |
| 2 | | | | | |
| 3 | | | | | |
| 4 | | | | | |
| 5 | | | | | |
| 6 | | | | | |
| 7 | | | | | |
| 8 | | | | | |
| 9 | | | | | |
| 10 | | | | | |
| 11 | | | | | |

**2** A manufacturing business has produced 330,000 of its product in the quarter ending 30 June 2003 at a total manufacturing cost of £567,900. The budgeted production for the quarter had been 350,000 units and the actual hours worked in the quarter were 12,600.

In the quarter ending 31 March 2003 the budgeted production was 320,000 units and actual product was 332,000 units. This production level was achieved in 12,300 hours and the total cost of production in the quarter was £580,400.

Tabulate this information on a computer spreadsheet and insert appropriate formulae in order that the following performance indicators can be calculated for each quarter:

i) cost per unit
ii) labour productivity
iii) productivity index

| | A | B | C | D | E |
|---|---|---|---|---|---|
| 1 | | | | | |
| 2 | | | | | |
| 3 | | | | | |
| 4 | | | | | |
| 5 | | | | | |
| 6 | | | | | |
| 7 | | | | | |
| 8 | | | | | |
| 9 | | | | | |
| 10 | | | | | |
| 11 | | | | | |

3 Given below are the sales figures for a business for each of the last six months.

| | *Feb* | *Mar* | *Apr* | *May* | *June* | *July* |
|---|---|---|---|---|---|---|
| | £'000 | £'000 | £'000 | £'000 | £'000 | £'000 |
| Sales | 320 | 300 | 360 | 400 | 350 | 310 |

You are to show these sales figures in a simple bar chart.

4 Given below are the summarised profit and loss figures for a business for the last three years:

| | *30 June 2001* | *30 June 2002* | *30 June 2003* |
|---|---|---|---|
| | £'000 | £'000 | £'000 |
| Sales | 280 | 350 | 400 |
| Cost of sales | 175 | 200 | 220 |
| Gross profit | 105 | 150 | 180 |
| Expenses | 60 | 70 | 80 |
| Net profit | 45 | 80 | 100 |

Show the sales, gross profit and net profit for each of the three years in a compound bar chart.

5 Given below are the sales figures for each of the three divisions of a company for the last four quarters.

| | *To 30 Sept 2002* | *To 31 Dec 2002* | *To 31 Mar 2003* | *To 30 June 2003* |
|---|---|---|---|---|
| | £'000 | £'000 | £'000 | £'000 |
| Division A | 160 | 180 | 220 | 250 |
| Division B | 150 | 120 | 100 | 100 |
| Division C | 120 | 140 | 150 | 170 |
| | 430 | 440 | 470 | 520 |

You are to show the sales for each division for each quarter in a component bar chart.

**6** Given below are the profit figures for three hotels owned by a business for the last three years:

| | *2001* | *2002* | *2003* |
|---|---|---|---|
| | £'000 | £'000 | £'000 |
| Royal Hotel | 320 | 350 | 300 |
| Mermaid Hotel | 110 | 70 | 50 |
| Crown Hotel | 290 | 340 | 320 |

You are to illustrate these figures in the following ways:

i) show the total profit for the three years in a simple bar chart
ii) show the breakdown of profit between the hotels in a compound bar chart
iii) show the breakdown of the profit between the hotels in a component bar chart

**7** Given below is a breakdown of the costs of a manufacturing business for the last three months:

| | *May* | *June* | *July* |
|---|---|---|---|
| | £'000 | £'000 | £'000 |
| Production costs | 400 | 500 | 460 |
| Selling and distribution costs | 120 | 250 | 160 |
| Administration costs | 100 | 140 | 180 |
| Finance costs | 50 | 50 | 150 |
| | 670 | 940 | 950 |

You are to illustrate the breakdown of these costs in a pie chart for each of the three months.

# chapter 14:
# REPORTING FIGURES OVER TIME

1 Given below are the number of customers served in a restaurant each day for the last 7 days:

| | |
|---|---|
| Sunday | 159 |
| Monday | 62 |
| Tuesday | 55 |
| Wednesday | 86 |
| Thursday | 104 |
| Friday | 168 |
| Saturday | 192 |

What is the average number of customers each day?

2 Given below are the monthly sales figures for a business for the last year:

| | £ |
|---|---|
| July 2002 | 337,600 |
| August 2002 | 415,300 |
| September 2002 | 289,500 |
| October 2002 | 266,400 |
| November 2002 | 198,700 |
| December 2002 | 258,600 |
| January 2003 | 177,200 |
| February 2003 | 199,300 |
| March 2003 | 222,900 |
| April 2003 | 256,100 |
| May 2003 | 265,800 |
| June 2003 | 365,700 |

Calculate a three month moving average for these sales figures.

**3** Given below are the weekly production costs for the first 16 weeks of the year for a manufacturing business:

| *Week* | *Costs* |
|---|---|
| | £ |
| 1 | 128,500 |
| 2 | 195,400 |
| 3 | 148,600 |
| 4 | 177,800 |
| 5 | 137,500 |
| 6 | 165,700 |
| 7 | 148,200 |
| 8 | 183,400 |
| 9 | 177,300 |
| 10 | 164,700 |
| 11 | 155,400 |
| 12 | 193,600 |
| 13 | 158,100 |
| 14 | 174,500 |
| 15 | 162,900 |
| 16 | 159,400 |

Calculate a four week moving average for these production figures.

**4** Using the figures from the previous activity prepare a computer spreadsheet to calculate the four week moving average.

| | A | B | C | D |
|---|---|---|---|---|
| 1 | | | | |
| 2 | | | | |
| 3 | | | | |
| 4 | | | | |
| 5 | | | | |
| 6 | | | | |
| 7 | | | | |
| 8 | | | | |
| 9 | | | | |
| 10 | | | | |
| 11 | | | | |
| 12 | | | | |
| 13 | | | | |
| 14 | | | | |
| 15 | | | | |
| 16 | | | | |
| 17 | | | | |
| 18 | | | | |
| 19 | | | | |
| 20 | | | | |
| 21 | | | | |
| 22 | | | | |
| 23 | | | | |
| 24 | | | | |
| 25 | | | | |
| 26 | | | | |
| 27 | | | | |
| 28 | | | | |
| 29 | | | | |
| 30 | | | | |
| 31 | | | | |

**5** Given below are the monthly production cost figures for a small manufacturing business:

| *2002* | £ |
|---|---|
| January | 55,600 |
| February | 52,700 |
| March | 56,100 |
| April | 56,800 |
| May | 58,300 |
| June | 60,500 |
| July | 58,900 |
| August | 59,200 |
| September | 61,300 |
| October | 62,100 |
| November | 63,400 |
| December | 62,700 |
| *2003* | |
| January | 61,300 |
| February | 62,500 |
| March | 64,100 |
| April | 65,200 |
| May | 64,900 |
| June | 66,700 |

You are required to:

i) calculate a three month moving average in order to show the trend of these figures
ii) plot the monthly figures and the trend line on a graph.

**6** Explain the difference between interpolation and extrapolation.

7 Given below are the sales figures for a business for the last year:

| | |
|---|---|
| 2002 | £ |
| August | 527,500 |
| September | 513,400 |
| October | 556,700 |
| November | 523,400 |
| December | 582,300 |
| 2003 | |
| January | 561,300 |
| February | 532,600 |
| March | 524,300 |
| April | 515,700 |
| May | 529,600 |
| June | 538,200 |

Using August 2002 as the base month with an index of 100 show the index for each of the subsequent month's sales.

**8** Given below are the sales for a business for the first 8 months of the year together with the Retail Price Index for that month:

| | | £ | RPI |
|---|---|---|---|
| January | 162400 | 162,400 | 171.1 |
| February | 162943 | 163,800 | 172.0 |
| March | 164846 | 165,900 | 172.2 |
| April | 165364 | 167,200 | 173.0 |
| May | 165234 | 166,200 | 172.1 |
| June | 163908 | 164,100 | 171.3 |
| July | 162395 | 162,300 | 171.0 |
| August | 161254 | 160,500 | 170.3 |

a) Calculate the RPI adjusted sales figures for the 8 months with prices being reflected in terms of January prices.

b) Using the RPI adjusted sales figures produce an index for the sales for each month with January as the base period.

c) Prepare a computer spreadsheet which will calculate the RPI adjusted index by inserting appropriate formulae.

| | A | B | C | D | E |
|---|---|---|---|---|---|
| 1 | | | | | |
| 2 | | | | | |
| 3 | | | | | |
| 4 | | | | | |
| 5 | | | | | |
| 6 | | | | | |
| 7 | | | | | |
| 8 | | | | | |

# chapter 15: EXTERNAL REPORTING

1 Name as many of the 'themes' included in the government's National Statistics as you can remember.

2 Given below is a grant application form for a grant from the local authority:

**BARDEN LOCAL DISTRICT COUNCIL**
**GRANT APPLICATION**

**PART 1 BUSINESS DETAILS**

Business name ..................................................

..................................................

Business address ..................................................

..................................................

..................................................

Business telephone ..................................................

Business fax ..................................................

Owner's name ..................................................

..................................................

Type of business ..................................................

..................................................

..................................................

..................................................

# PART 2 FINANCIAL DETAILS

## 2A TURNOVER AND PROFIT

Figures are to be provided for annual turnover and reported net profit for the last three complete financial years

| Financial year ended: | UK turnover £ | Export turnover £ | Net profit £ |
|---|---|---|---|
| Month Year | | | |

## 2B WORKING CAPITAL

Figures are to be provided for working capital at the end of the most recent financial year.

Year ending:

| | £ |
|---|---|
| Current assets | ..................... |
| Minus: current liabilities | ..................... |
| Working capital | ..................... |

## 2C FIXED ASSETS

Figures are to be provided for fixed asset totals at the end of the most recent financial year.

Year ending:

| | £ |
|---|---|
| Land and buildings | ..................... |
| Plant and machinery | ..................... |
| Other | ..................... |
| Total fixed assets | ..................... |

## PART 3 NON FINANCIAL DETAILS

### 3A EMPLOYMENT DETAILS

Figures are to be provided for the number of employees for the last three financial years.

| Financial year ended: | Number of full time employees | Number of part time employees |
|---|---|---|
| Month Year | | |

### 3B BUSINESS DETAILS

Date business started: ..........................................................

Business type - Sole trader ☐

Partnership ☐

Company ☐

## PART 4 GRANT APPLICATION

Indicate in the space provided the reasons for the grant application. If the grant application is processed further more detail will be requested at a later date.

..........................................................................................

..........................................................................................

..........................................................................................

..........................................................................................

..........................................................................................

..........................................................................................

..........................................................................................

You work for a partnership called D & G Harper which was set up in 1994 by David and Gareth Harper to manufacture curtains and blinds largely for businesses. The business is run on a day to day basis by David Harper and in the year ended 30 June 2003 employed 14 full time employees and 3 part-time employees. The business expanded in the year ended 30 June 2002 and in that year 5 more full time employees were taken on and 2 part -time employees.

The grant application is for £15,000 to help fund additional factory space and the potential employment of potentially 6 additional full time employees.

The business is run from Harper House, East Park Road, Barden, BD4 6GK and the telephone number and fax number are 02185 3743 and 02185 3264 respectively.

You have been asked to complete the grant application form prior to it being signed and checked by David Harper. From the accounting records you have been able to find summaries of the profit and loss accounts for the last three years and a summarised balance sheet as at 30 June 2003.

**Summarised profit and loss accounts**

| | *Y/e 30 June 2001* | *Y/e 30 June 2002* | *Y/e 30 June 2003* |
|---|---|---|---|
| | £ | £ | £ |
| UK sales | 378,690 | 735,400 | 882,400 |
| Export sales | 10,580 | 38,600 | 48,340 |
| | 389,270 | 774,000 | 930,740 |
| Cost of sales | 210,580 | 387,400 | 446,750 |
| | 178,690 | 386,600 | 483,990 |
| Expenses | 104,580 | 224,060 | 279,220 |
| Net profit | 74,110 | 162,540 | 204,770 |

**Summarised balance sheet as at 30 June 2003**

| | £ | £ | £ |
|---|---|---|---|
| Fixed assets: | | | |
| Land and buildings | | | 184,500 |
| Machinery | | | 190,400 |
| Cars | | | 84,500 |
| Office equipment | | | 13,200 |
| | | | 472,600 |
| Current assets: | | | |
| Stock of fabrics | | 28,400 | |
| Debtors | | 65,400 | |
| Cash at bank | | 3,670 | |
| | | 97,470 | |
| Current liabilities: | | | |
| Trade creditors | 38,600 | | |
| PAYE/NIC | 3,570 | | |
| | | 42,170 | |
| | | | 55,300 |
| | | | 527,900 |

You are required to complete the grant application form ready for checking and signature.

3 You work as an accounting technician for a medium sized building firm with a turnover for the year ended 30 June 2003 of £367,400 and for the previous year turnover of £283,400. The net profit made in the year ended 30 June 2003 was £48,414 compared to £39,382 for the previous year. The owner of the business is confident that turnover and profits will continue to increase in the foreseeable future. All of the business takes place in the UK.

You are required to complete the Chamber of Commerce Annual Economic Review that has been sent to your business in order to aid in the collection of National Statistics.

## CHAMBER OF COMMERCE
## ANNUAL ECONOMIC REVIEW

Please tick the appropriate box in answer to each question – all answers will be treated in the strictest confidence. All answers should be based upon the business performance for the last full financial year.

### 1 BUSINESS DETAILS

End of last full financial year:

Turnover range:

| | |
|---|---|
| Upto £50,000 | ☐ |
| £50,000 - £100,000 | ☐ |
| £100,000 - £250,000 | ☐ |
| £250,000 - £500,000 | ☐ |
| £500,000 - £1,000,000 | ☐ |
| Over £1,000,000 | ☐ |

Main business activity:

| | | | |
|---|---|---|---|
| Engineering | ☐ | Health | ☐ |
| Construction | ☐ | Art and design | ☐ |
| Agriculture | ☐ | Transport | ☐ |
| Energy | ☐ | Tourism | ☐ |
| Retail | ☐ | Other (please state) . . . . . . . . . . | |
| Education | ☐ | . . . . . . . . . . . . . . . . . . . . . . . . | |

**2 TURNOVER**

Percentage of total turnover accounted for by export sales:

| | | | |
|---|---|---|---|
| 0% | ☐ | 30% to 50% | ☐ |
| up to 10% | ☐ | 50% to 75% | ☐ |
| 10% to 20% | ☐ | 75% to 100% | ☐ |
| 20% to 30% | ☐ | | |

Percentage increase/decrease in turnover compared to previous financial year:

| | | | |
|---|---|---|---|
| Decrease upto 20% | ☐ | Increase upto 20% | ☐ |
| Decrease of 20% to 50% | ☐ | Increase of 20% to 50% | ☐ |
| Decrease of more than 50% | ☐ | Increase of more than 50% | ☐ |

Percentage increase/decrease in net profit compared to previous financial year:

| | | | |
|---|---|---|---|
| Decrease upto 20% | ☐ | Increase upto 20% | ☐ |
| Decrease of 20% to 50% | ☐ | Increase of 20% to 50% | ☐ |
| Decrease of more than 50% | ☐ | Increase of more than 50% | ☐ |

**3 BUSINESS CONFIDENCE**

Do you consider that over the following 12 months:

| | | | | | |
|---|---|---|---|---|---|
| Turnover | will increase | ☐ | Profitability | will increase | ☐ |
| | remain the same | ☐ | | remain the same | ☐ |
| | decrease | ☐ | | decrease | ☐ |

# chapter 16: VALUE ADDED TAX

**1** Complete the following sentences:

i) From 1 April 2004 the VAT registration threshold is £ ~~80,000~~ 58,000

ii) From 1 April 2004 the VAT deregistration limit is £ 56,000

iii) VAT on purchases is known as Input tax

iv) VAT on sales is known as Output tax

v) A VAT return is normally completed every 3 months

**2** What are the three rates of VAT in the UK currently?

EXEMPT - 0

STANDARD - 17·5.

Reduced - 5.

**3** A business has made purchases during a month of £13,500 plus VAT. What is the total cost of these purchases for each of the following businesses and why? £15862·50 - CANNOT Reclaim

i) a business that makes exempt supplies ~~£13,500 NO VAT CHARGED~~ VAT

ii) a business that makes zero-rated supplies £13,500 0 Rate VAT - Can Reclaim.

**4** Why might a business register for VAT even if its turnover has not reached the VAT registration limit?

**5** A VAT registered business has made the following purchases:

i) A car for use by a business salesman for £14,200 plus VAT
ii) A business lunch for clients costing £120 plus VAT.

What is the cost to the business of each of these expenses and why?

£16,685 ~~£14,200~~ - CARS ARE EXEMPT - NOT Reclaimable.

£141 - Charge VAT. - Cannot Reclaim

**6** What is the tax point in each of the following situations and is it a basic tax point or an actual tax point?

i) An invoice is dispatched to a customer on 13 August 2003 and the goods are delivered the following day. 13 AUG - ACTUAL TAX POINT.

ii) Goods are delivered on 15 August 2003 and the invoice is sent to the customer on 31 August 2003 15 AUG - ACTUAL TAX POINT

iii) Services are provided to a customer on 8 August 2003 and an invoice is sent out on 12 August 2003. 8 AUG - ACT

iv) A customer pays for goods on 20 August 2003 and the goods are delivered two days later.

20 AUG

**7** Calculate the amount of VAT that should be charged in each of the following situations:

i) goods sold for £146.80 plus VAT £25.69

ii) goods sold for £220.00 plus VAT less a trade discount of 10% £34.65.

iii) goods sold for £200.00 plus VAT with a settlement discount of 3% offered £33.95.

iv) goods sold for £320.00 plus VAT less a trade discount of 20% and a settlement discount of 2%

~~£43.51~~ £43.90.

64
6.40

**8** Calculate the VAT and the net of VAT amount in each of the following:

| | | | |
|---|---|---|---|
| i) | £432.16 including VAT | £367.80. | £64.36. |
| ii) | £262.77 including VAT | £223.63 | £39.14. |
| iii) | £216.90 including VAT | £184.60 | £32.30. |
| iv) | £310.18 including VAT | £263.98 | £46.20. |

**9** Explain what details would appear on a less detailed VAT invoice for a retail sale of less than £100.00.

Creditor Address, Debtor address, Product detail, Net, Gross + VAT figure.

# chapter 17: VAT RECORDS

1 Given below is information about the VAT of a business that has been taken from the books of prime entry:

**VAT figures**

| | £ |
|---|---|
| From the sales day book | 3,474.89 |
| From the sales returns day book | 441.46 |
| From the purchases day book | 2,485.61 |
| From the purchases returns day book | 210.68 |
| From the cash receipts book | 993.57 |
| From the cash payments book | 624.78 |
| EU acquisitions | 925.47 |

Write up the VAT control account.

VAT account

| | £ | | £ |
|---|---|---|---|
| SRDB | 441.46. | SDB | 3474.89. |
| PDB | 2485.61 | PRDB | 210.68. |
| CRB | 993.57 | CPB | 624.78. |

**2** Given below is information about the VAT of a business taken from the books of prime entry:

| | £ |
|---|---:|
| From the sales day book | 6,275.78 |
| From the sales returns day book | 726.58 |
| From the purchases day book | 4,668.14 |
| From the purchases returns day book | 510.36 |
| From the cash receipts book | 1,447.30 |
| From the cash payments book | 936.47 |
| EU acquisitions | 772.46 |
| Bad debt relief | 284.67 |
| VAT underpaid in a previous period | 126.57 |
| VAT overpaid in a previous period | 221.68 |

You are to write up the VAT control account.

Input                                        Output.

VAT account

| | £ | | £ |
|---|---:|---|---:|
| PDB | 4668.14 | SDB | 6275.78 |
| CRB | 1447.30 | CPB | 936.47 |
| EU Aq | 772.46 | EU Aq | 772.46 |
| Bad Debt | 284.67 | VAT u/p | 126.57 |
| VAT o/p | 221.68 | | |
| | 7394.25 | | 8111.28 |
| Less CN Rec | (726.58) | Less CN out | (510 36 |
| | 6667.67 | | 7600.92 |

**3** Given below are extracts from the books of prime entry for a business Waltzer Enterprises, Adam Industrial Park, Yarden, LR3 9GS. The business's VAT registration number is 234 4576 12 and the tax period is April 2003 to June 2003.

**Sales day book summary**

| | *Zero-rated sales* | *Standard rated sales* | *VAT* | *Total* |
|---|---|---|---|---|
| | £ | £ | £ | £ |
| Total | 3,628.47 | 57,615.80 | 10,082.76 | 71,327.03 |

**Purchases day book summary**

| | *Zero-rated purchases* | *Standard rated purchases* | *VAT* | *Total* |
|---|---|---|---|---|
| | £ | £ | £ | £ |
| EU acquisitions | | 1,572.45 | 275.17 | 1,847.62 |
| UK purchases | 2,636.47 | 33,672.57 | 5,892.69 | 42,201.73 |

**Sales returns day book summary**

| | *Zero-rated sales* | *Standard rated sales* | *VAT* | *Total* |
|---|---|---|---|---|
| | £ | £ | £ | £ |
| Total | 236.34 | 4,782.57 | 836.94 | 5,855.85 |

**Purchases returns day book summary**

| | *Zero-rated purchases* | *Standard rated purchases* | *VAT* | *Total* |
|---|---|---|---|---|
| | £ | £ | £ | £ |
| Total | 125.34 | 3,184.57 | 557.29 | 3,867.20 |

**Cash receipts book summary**

| | *Net* | *VAT* | *Total* |
|---|---|---|---|
| | £ | £ | £ |
| Cash sales | 5,325.65 | 931.98 | 6,257.63 |

**Cash payments book summary**

| | *Net* | *VAT* | *Total* |
|---|---|---|---|
| | £ | £ | £ |
| Cash purchases | 3,157.46 | 552.55 | 3,710.01 |

You are required to complete the VAT return given.

**Value Added Tax Return**

For the period
01 04 01 to 30 06 01

For Official Use

Registration number: 234 4576 12

Period: 02/03

You could be liable to a financial penalty if your completed return and all the VAT payable are not received by the due date.

Due date:

For Official Use

If you have a general enquiry or need advice please call our National Advice Service on 0845 010 9000

**ATTENTION**

If this return and any tax due are not received by the due date you may be liable to a surcharge.

If you make supplies of goods to another EC Member State you are required to complete an EC Sales List (VAT 101).

Before you fill in this form please read the notes on the back and the VAT Leaflet *"Filling in your VAT return"*. Fill in all boxes clearly in ink, and write 'none' where necessary. Don't put a dash or leave any box blank. If there are no pence write "00" in the pence column. Do not enter more than one amount in any box.

For official use

| | Box | £ | p |
|---|---|---|---|
| VAT due in this period on sales and other outputs | 1 | 10177 | 80 |
| VAT due in this period on acquisitions from other EC Member States | 2 | 275 | 17 |
| Total VAT due (the sum of boxes 1 and 2) | 3 | 10,452 | 97 |
| VAT reclaimed in this period on purchases and other inputs (including acquisitions from the EC) | 4 | 6163 | 12 |
| **Net VAT to be paid to Customs or reclaimed by you (Difference between boxes 3 and 4)** | 5 | 4262 | 85 |
| Total value of sales and all other outputs excluding any VAT. Include your box 8 figure | 6 | 61244 | 00 |
| Total value of purchases and all other inputs excluding any VAT. Include your box 9 figure | 7 | 37831 | 00 |
| Total value of all supplies of goods and related services, excluding any VAT, to other EC Member States | 8 | NONE | 00 |
| Total value of all acquisitions of goods and related services, excluding any VAT, from other EC Member States | 9 | 1572 | 00 |

If you are enclosing a payment please tick this box.

DECLARATION: You, or someone on your behalf, must sign below.

I, .................................................................... declare that the
(Full name of signatory in BLOCK LETTERS)
information given above is true and complete.

Signature.......................................................... Date ................................

**A false declaration can result in prosecution.**

**4** What would you do if you discovered that your business had made an error on an earlier VAT return which was more than £2,000?

..............................................................................................................................

..............................................................................................................................

..............................................................................................................................

..............................................................................................................................

..............................................................................................................................

..............................................................................................................................

**5** Explain how the annual accounting scheme for VAT works.

..............................................................................................................................

..............................................................................................................................

..............................................................................................................................

..............................................................................................................................

..............................................................................................................................

..............................................................................................................................

..............................................................................................................................

..............................................................................................................................

..............................................................................................................................

..............................................................................................................................

..............................................................................................................................

..............................................................................................................................

..............................................................................................................................

..............................................................................................................................

..............................................................................................................................

..............................................................................................................................

..............................................................................................................................

..............................................................................................................................

..............................................................................................................................

# PRACTICE EXAM BASED ASSESSMENT 1 UNIT 6

## SPORTS LTD

**These tasks were set by the AAT in December 2003.**

**Time allowed: 3 hours plus 15 minutes reading time**

This examination paper is in TWO sections.

You have to show competence in BOTH sections.

You should therefore attempt and aim to complete EVERY task in BOTH sections.

You should spend about 90 minutes on each section.

All essential workings should be included within your answers where appropriate.

Both sections are based on Sports Ltd.

# SECTION 1 (Suggested time allowance: 90 minutes)

## DATA

Sports Ltd manufactures and sells sporting goods. You work as an accounting technician at Sports Ltd, reporting to the Finance Director.

The company's most popular product is a leather football.

The company operates an integrated absorption costing system. Stocks are valued on a first in first out (FIFO) basis.

The Finance Director has given you the following tasks.

## Task 1.1

Complete the following stock card for leather using the FIFO method for valuing issues to production and stocks of materials.

| STOCK CARD | | | | | | | | |
|---|---|---|---|---|---|---|---|---|
| **Product:** | **Leather** | | | | | | | |
| | *Receipts* | | | *Issues* | | | *Balance* | |
| *Date* | *Quantity (metres)* | *Cost (per metre) £* | *Total Cost £* | *Quantity (metres)* | *Cost (per metre) £* | *Total Cost £* | *Quantity (metres)* | *Total Cost £* |
| B/f at 1 Nov | | | | | | | 10,000 | 10,000 |
| 5 Nov | 15,000 | 1.20 | 18,000 | | | | 25,000 | 28,000 |
| 12 Nov | | | | 10,000 | 1-00 | 10,000 | 15000 | 18,000 |
| 19 Nov | 10,000 | 1.10 | 11000 | | | | 25000 | 29000 |
| 26 Nov | | | | 20,000 | 15 1-20<br>5 1-10 | 18000<br>5500 | 5000 | 5500 |

## ADDITIONAL DATA

Leather stocks are only used for the manufacture of leather footballs. The following cost accounting codes are used to record material costs:

| *Code number* | *Description* |
|---|---|
| 1000 | Leather stocks |
| 1100 | Work in progress - leather footballs |
| 3000 | Creditors control |

### Task 1.2

Complete the table below to show how the two purchases and two issues of leather would be recorded in the cost accounting records.

| *Date* | *Code* | *Dr* | *Cr* |
|---|---|---|---|
| 5 November | 1000 | 18000 | |
| 5 November | 3000 | | 18000 |
| 12 November | 1100 | 10000 | |
| 12 November | 1000 | | 10000 |
| 19 November | 1000 | 11000 | |
| 19 November | 3000 | | 11000 |
| 26 November | 1100 | 23500 | |
| 26 November | 1000 | | 23500 |

## ADDITIONAL DATA

Direct labour overtime payments are included in direct costs. The following data relates to the production of leather footballs for November:

| | |
|---|---|
| Total direct labour hours worked | 9,500 hours |
| Normal time hours | 8,800 hours |
| Overtime hours | 700 hours |
| Normal time rate per hour | £5 per hour |
| Overtime premium per hour | £2 per hour |

### Task 1.3

Calculate the total cost of direct labour for November.

9500 @ 5 = 47500   8800 @ 5 = 44000

700 @ 7   4900   = 48900

# ADDITIONAL DATA

Production comprises three departments:

- Cutting
- Finishing
- Maintenance

The budgeted and actual fixed production overheads of the company for November were as follows:

| | £ |
|---|---|
| Machine insurance | 6,000 |
| Rent and other property overheads | 17,100 |
| Power costs: | |
| Cutting | 600 |
| Finishing | 1,050 |
| Maintenance | 150 |
| Indirect staff costs: | |
| Cutting | 5,940 |
| Finishing | 4,770 |
| Maintenance | 9,540 |
| Total budgeted and actual fixed production overheads | 45,150 |

The following information is also relevant:

| *Department* | *Floor space occupied* (square metres) | *Net book value of fixed assets* £000 |
|---|---|---|
| Cutting | 6,000 | 20 |
| Finishing | 3,000 | 25 |
| Maintenance | 1,000 | 5 |

Overheads are allocated and apportioned using the most appropriate method. The total maintenance overheads are then reapportioned to the cutting and finishing department. The maintenance records show that 40% of time is spent in the cutting department and 60% in the finishing department.

## Task 1.4

Complete the following table showing the allocation and apportionment of fixed overheads between the three departments.

| *Fixed overheads for November* | *Basis* | *Total* £ | *Cutting* £ | *Finishing* £ | *Maintenance* £ |
|---|---|---|---|---|---|
| Machine insurance | net | 6,000 | 2400 | 3000 | 600 |
| Rent and other property overheads | SQ | 17,100 | 10260 | 5130 | 1710 |
| Power costs | Allocate | 1,800 | 600 | 1050 | 150 |
| Staff costs | Allocated | 20,250 | 5940 | 4770 | 9540 |
| | | 45,150 | 19200 | 13950 | 12000 |
| Maintenance | | | 4800 | 7200 | (12000) |
| | | 45,150 | 24000 | 21150 | |

## ADDITIONAL DATA

Cutting department fixed overheads are absorbed on the basis of budgeted direct labour hours. Finishing department fixed overheads are absorbed on the basis of budgeted machine hours. The following information relates to the cutting and finishing departments for November.

- The budgeted number of direct labour hours in the cutting department was 9,600 hours.
- The budgeted number of machine hours in the finishing department was 7,050 hours.
- The actual direct labour hours worked in the cutting department were 9,250 hours.
- The actual machine hours worked in the finishing department were 7,350 hours.

## Task 1.5

Use the data from task 1.4 to calculate the budgeted fixed overhead absorption rates for November for:

(a) the cutting department

£2.50 24000 ÷ 9600

(b) the finishing department.

£3.00

## Task 1.6

Use the information from tasks 1.4 and 1.5 to:

(a) Calculate the production overhead absorbed for November in:

(i) the cutting department

actual labour hrs

23125 (9250 x 2.50)

(ii) the finishing department.

actual machine hrs

22050 (7350 X3

(b) Calculate the under or over absorbed production overheads for November, indicating clearly whether the overheads are under or over absorbed for:

(i) the cutting department

under by 875

(ii) the finishing department.

over 900

(c) Explain how the under or over absorbed production overheads for the cutting and finishing departments will be recorded in the profit and loss account for November.

over will debit p+l and credit wip

Under will credit p+l and debit wip

# SECTION 2 (Suggested time allowance: 90 minutes)

## DATA

In addition to producing leather footballs, the company is considering producing three types of running shoes, products Exe, Wye and Zed. Expected monthly costs and sales information for each product are as follows.

| *Product* | *Exe* | *Wye* | *Zed* |
|---|---|---|---|
| Sales and production units | 2,000 | 3,000 | 5,000 |
| Labour hours per month | 1,000 | 1,200 | 2,000 |
| Unit selling price | £30.00 | £25.00 | £20.00 |
| Unit material cost | £10.00 | £8.00 | £6.00 |
| Unit direct labour cost | £2.50 | £2.00 | £2.00 |
| Unit contribution | £17.50 | £15.00 | £12.00 |

The total expected monthly fixed costs relating to the production of running shoes are £32,000.

## Task 2.1

Complete the table below to calculate the forecast monthly total contribution and profit for the company from the sale and production of running shoes.

unit cost × units

| *Product* | *Exe* £ | *Wye* £ | *Zed* £ | *Total* £ |
|---|---|---|---|---|
| Sales revenue | 60000 | 75000 | 100,000. | 235 000 |
| Less: Variable costs | | | | |
| Direct materials | 20'000 | 24'000 | 30'000 | 74000 |
| Direct labour | 5000 | 6000 | 10'000 | 21000 |
| Total contribution | 35'000 | 45000 | 60'000 | 140'000 |
| Fixed overheads | | | | 32'000 |
| Forecast profit | | | | 108'000 |

## ADDITIONAL DATA

For this task, assume the company only manufactures product Exe. It does not manufacture products Wye and Zed.

### Task 2.2

(a) Complete the table below for both production volumes.

| *Product: Exe* | *Production volume* | |
|---|---|---|
| | 1,600 units | 2,000 units |
| Monthly variable costs | 20'000 | 25'000 |
| Monthly fixed costs | 32 000 | 32'000 |
| Total cost of production | 52'000 | 57'000 |
| Unit cost of production | 32-50 | 28-50 |

(b) Calculate the number of units of product Exe that the company would need to make and sell each month to make a profit of £2,000.

fixed + profit intended ÷ contribution 17-50

## ADDITIONAL DATA

For each of the next three months, the Production Director estimates that there is a maximum of 3,000 direct labour hours available for the production of running shoes.

### Task 2.3

(a) Use the data from task 2.1 to complete the table below.

| *Product* | *Exe* | *Wye* | *Zed* |
|---|---|---|---|
| Unit contribution | 17-50 | 15-00 | 12-00 |
| Labour hours per unit | 0.5 | 0.4 | 0.4 |
| Contribution per labour hour | 35 | 37-50 | 30 |

(b) Calculate how many units of products Exe, Wye and Zed the company should make and sell each month to maximise its profits using 3,000 labour hours.

## ADDITIONAL DATA

The company requires an annual rate of return of 10% on any new project. The Managing Director has asked you to appraise the long-term financial effects of producing sports clothing. You are given the following information relating to this product.

| | *Year 0* | *Year 1* | *Year 2* | *Year 3* | *Year 4* |
|---|---|---|---|---|---|
| | £000 | £000 | £000 | £000 | £000 |
| Capital expenditure | 500 | | | | |
| Sales revenues | | 200 | 500 | 800 | 200 |
| Variable costs | | 140 | 350 | 480 | 120 |
| 10% Present value factor | 1.000 | 0.909 | 0.826 | 0.751 | 0.683 |

(500) 60 150 320 80
500 (440) (290) 30 50

## Task 2.4

Calculate for the sports clothing project:

(a) the payback period

..........................................................................................................................................

..........................................................................................................................................

(b) the net present value

| | *Year 0* | *Year 1* | *Year 2* | *Year 3* | *Year 4* |
|---|---|---|---|---|---|
| | £000 | £000 | £000 | £000 | £000 |
| Net cashflows | 500 | 60 | 150 | 320 | 80 |
| Present value factors | 1.000 | 0.909 | 0.826 | 0.751 | 0.683 |
| Present values | (500) | 54-54 | 123.90 | 240-32 | 54-64 |
| Net Present Value | (26-60) | | | | |

## Task 2.5

Use the data from task 2.4 to prepare a memo to the Managing Director on the sports clothing project. Your memo should:

(a) recommend whether to accept or reject the project, based on its net present value.

(b) identify TWO additional items of information relevant to appraising this project.

Use the memo paper on the next page.

## MEMO

**To:** Managing Director **Subject:**

**From:** **Date:**

# PRACTICE EXAM BASED ASSESSMENT 2 UNIT 6

# PLUMP LTD

**These tasks were set by the AAT in June 2003 and have been adapted to reflect the Revised Standards of Competence.**

**Time allowed: 3 hours plus 15 minutes reading time**

This examination paper is in TWO sections.

You have to show competence in BOTH sections.

You should therefore attempt and aim to complete EVERY task in BOTH sections.

You should spend about 90 minutes on each section.

All essential workings should be included within your answers where appropriate.

Both sections are based on Plump Ltd.

# SECTION 1 (Suggested time allowance: 90 minutes)

## DATA

Plump Ltd manufactures and sells clothes. You work as an accounting technician at Plump Ltd, reporting to the Finance Director.

The company's main product is a range of jackets made from cloth and lining fabric.

The company operates an integrated absorption costing system. Stocks are valued on an average cost (AVCO) basis. A new weighted average cost, correct to the nearest penny, is calculated each time a new delivery of stock is received.

The Finance Director has given you the following tasks.

## Task 1.1

Complete the following stock card for black cloth for May 2003.

| STOCK CARD | | | | | | | | | |
|---|---|---|---|---|---|---|---|---|---|
| **Product:** | **Black cloth** | | | | | | | | |
| | *Receipts* | | | *Issues* | | | *Balance* | | |
| *Date* | *Quantity (metres)* | *Cost per metre* £ | *Total cost* £ | *Quantity (metres)* | *Cost per metre* £ | *Total cost* £ | *Quantity (metres)* | *Cost per metre* £ | *Total cost* £ |
| B/f at 1 May | | | | | | | 12,000 | 5.00 | 60,000 |
| 4 May | 10,000 | 5.44 | 54'400 | | | | 22,000 | 5-44 | 114400 |
| 6 May | | | | 13,500 | 5-20 | 70 200 | 8500 | 5-20 | 44400 |
| 16 May | 15,000 | 5.36 | 80400 | | | | 23500 | 5-36 | 124800 |
| 21 May | | | | 18,200 | 5.30 | 96'642 | 5300 | 5-30 | 28158 |
| 30 May | 20,000 | 4.90 | 98000 | | | | 25300 | 4-90 | 126148 |

## ADDITIONAL DATA

The following cost accounting codes are used to record material costs:

| *Code number* | *Description* |
|---|---|
| 1030 | Black cloth |
| 1200 | Work in progress – jackets |
| 4000 | Creditors control account |

## Task 1.2

Complete the table below to show how the purchase on 4 May, and the issue on 6 May would be recorded in the cost account records.

| *Date* | *Code* | *Dr* £ | *Cr* £ |
|---|---|---|---|
| 4 May | 1030 | 54400 | |
| | | | 54400 |
| 6 May | 1200 | 70200 | |

70200

## ADDITIONAL DATA

The Payroll Summary for production workers for May is given below.

| | *Gross pay* | *PAYE* | *NI* | *Net pay* |
|---|---|---|---|---|
| | £ | £ | £ | £ |
| Direct labour | 120,000 | 27,000 | 9,300 | 83,700 |
| Indirect labour | 43,000 | 8,200 | 3,000 | 31,800 |
| Total | 163,000 | 35,200 | 12,300 | 115,500 |

Further account codes which are relevant to the payroll are:

| *Code number* | *Description* |
|---|---|
| 1180 | Production overheads |
| 3000 | Wages control |
| 4500 | Inland Revenue |
| 6000 | Cash at bank |

### Task 1.3

Record the payroll information for May in the wages control account given below.

**Wages control account**

| Date | Account code | Description | £ | Date | Account code | Description | £ |
|---|---|---|---|---|---|---|---|
| MAY | | | | | | | |
| | | | | | | | |

## ADDITIONAL DATA

Plump Ltd has the following departments.

- Warehouse
- Manufacturing
- Sales
- Accounting

The budgeted overheads of the company are all treated as fixed costs. The monthly budgeted overheads are as follows:

| | £ |
|---|---|
| Depreciation | 10,000 |
| Rent | 35,000 |
| Other property overheads | 12,500 |
| Staff costs: | |
| Warehousing | 2,800 |
| Manufacturing | 6,925 |
| Sales | 15,875 |
| Accounting | 14,050 |
| Other accounting overheads | 13,600 |
| Total monthly budgeted fixed overheads | 110,750 |

The following information is also relevant:

| *Department* | *% of floor space occupied* | *Net book value of fixed assets* |
|---|---|---|
| | | £000 |
| Warehouse | 20 | 100 |
| Manufacturing | 55 | 800 |
| Sales | 15 | 40 |
| Accounting | 10 | 60 |
| | 100 | 1,000 |

Overheads are allocated and apportioned between departments using the most appropriate basis. The total accounting overheads are then reapportioned to the other three departments using the following percentages.

*Apportionment of accounting department overheads*

- Warehouse 5%
- Manufacturing 65%
- Sales 30%

## Task 1.4

Complete the table below to show:

- the basis for allocation or apportionment of each overhead
- the allocation and apportionment of budgeted overheads between the four departments
- the reapportionment of the total accounting department overheads

| *Overhead* | *Basis* | *Total* £ | *Warehouse* £ | *Manufacturing* £ | *Sales* £ | *Accounting* £ |
|---|---|---|---|---|---|---|
| Depreciation | NBV | 10,000 | 1000 | 8000 | 400 | 600 |
| Rent | FLOOR SPACE | 35,000 | 7000 | 19250 | 5250 | 3500 |
| Other property overheads | FLOOR SPACE | 12,500 | 2500 | 6875 | | |
| Staff costs | ALLOCATED | 39,650 | | | | |
| Other accounting overheads | ALLOCATED | 13,600 | | | | |
| | | 110,750 | 13300 | 41050 | 23400 | 33000 |
| Accounting | | | 1650 | 21450 | 9900 | (33000) |
| | | 110,750 | 14950 | 62500 | 3300 | |

## ADDITIONAL DATA

Manufacturing fixed overheads are absorbed on the basis of budgeted direct labour hours. The following information is for the manufacturing department for May 2003.

- The budgeted number of direct labour hours was 25,000 hours.
- The actual direct labour hours worked were 26,500 hours.
- Actual fixed overheads were £66,300.

## Task 1.5

For the manufacturing department for May, calculate the budgeted fixed overhead absorption rate per direct labour hour.

.........2.50.........

..................................

## ADDITIONAL DATA

The company is considering expanding its manufacturing activities. It has two choices:

- Increase direct labour hours by 20%
- Increase direct labour hours by 30%

Any increase in activity will require additional machinery which will cost £120,000. This machinery will be depreciated over 10 years and will have no residual value at the end of its life.

## Task 1.6

Complete the table below for the manufacturing department showing:

(a) budgeted overheads for May (from Task 1.4);

(b) budgeted overheads for each increased activity level;

(c) the budgeted fixed overhead absorption rate per direct labour hour for each activity level.

| **Manufacturing department** | Budgeted activity (labour hours) | | |
|---|---|---|---|
| | 25,000 | 30,000 | 32,500 |
| Budgeted overheads | May<br>£ | £ | £ |
| Depreciation | [illegible] | [illegible] | [illegible] |
| Rent | 19250 | 19250 | 19250 |
| Other property overheads | 6875 | 6875 | 6875 |
| Staff costs | 6925 | 6925 | 6925. |
| Accounting | 21450 | 21450 | 21450 |
| Total | | | |
| Budgeted overhead absorption rate (rounded to nearest penny) | | | |

# ADDITIONAL DATA

The Finance Director is concerned about the current level of costs. He tells you that each jacket is budgeted to take 2 labour hours to manufacture and asks you to perform the following task.

## Task 1.7

Provide the budgeted overhead cost for the production of a black jacket for each of the activity levels described in Task 1.6.

| *Activity level* | £ |
|---|---|
| 25,000 labour hours | 242.50 |
| 30,000 labour hours | |
| 32,500 labour hours | |

# SECTION 2 (Suggested time allowance: 90 minutes)

## DATA

Plump Ltd has the opportunity to rent another business unit and is considering using it to produce a range of silk ties. A batch production system would operate, each batch comprising 1,000 ties. Demand for the ties is estimated at 20,000 per year, and the budget is to be based on this level of sales and production.

Estimated costs of each batch are as follows:

| | |
|---|---|
| Silk cloth | 200 metres at £7 per metre |
| Direct labour | 60 hours at £10 per hour |
| Packaging | £120 |
| Cutting machine running costs | The machine is to be treated as a cost centre and is estimated to attract variable overheads of £0.80 for each minute it is being used. Each batch requires 100 minutes of cutting machine time. |
| Other variable overheads | £3 per direct labour hour |
| Fixed overheads | £7.50 per direct labour hour |

### Task 2.1

Complete the table below to calculate the batch cost and the unit cost of production of the ties.

| | *Cost per batch* £ | *Cost per unit* £ |
|---|---|---|
| Direct materials – silk | 1400 | 1-40 |
| – packaging | 120 | 0-12 |
| Direct labour | 600 | 0 60 |
| Cutting machine running costs | 80 | 0.08 |
| Other variable overheads | 180 | 0·18 |
| Total variable costs | 2380 | 2-38. |
| Fixed overheads | 450· | 0.45. |
| Total cost | 2830 | 2-83. |

# ADDITIONAL DATA

The ties are to be sold to a retail chain for £5.50 each.

## Task 2.2

In relation to the new tie producing venture

(a) Calculate the contribution per unit.

5.50 – 2.38 = 3.12 ..........................................................................................

..........................................................................................

(b) Calculate the P/V ratio.

..........................................................................................

..........................................................................................

(c) Calculate the budgeted fixed costs per annum.

..........................................................................................

..........................................................................................

(d) Calculate the breakeven quantity, based on your contribution per unit figure, and comment on the validity of your answer.

..........................................................................................

..........................................................................................

(e) Complete the table below to calculate the budgeted profit resulting from the production and sale of ties over a one-year period

| | £ |
|---|---|
| Sales revenue (20,000 units) | 110 000 |
| Less: variable costs | 47600 |
| Total contribution | |
| Fixed overheads | 9000 |
| Forecast profit | |

(f) Complete the P/V chart below by marking on the position and values you have calculated for

(i) Fixed costs
(ii) Breakeven quantity
(iii) Profit at the budgeted level of sales

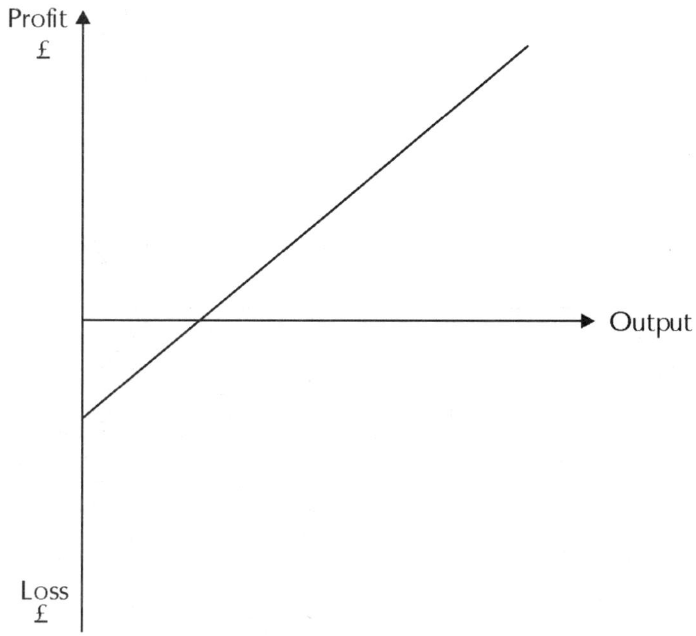


## Task 2.3

(a) Calculate the number of ties that would need to be sold in a year to make a profit of £70,000.

..............................................................................................................................

..............................................................................................................................

(b) If the maximum number of labour hours available in a year is 900, calculate the profit that would be made.

..............................................................................................................................

..............................................................................................................................

# ADDITIONAL DATA

There is some doubt as to whether the supply of silk cloth is reliable enough to proceed with this venture, so Plump Ltd is also considering using the new business unit for the production of trousers. Two lines have been costed:

| | *Casual* | *Luxury* |
|---|---|---|
| Contribution per unit | £16 | £24 |
| Maximum demand | 500 | 300 |

## Task 2.4

Complete the table below

| | *Casual* | *Luxury* |
|---|---|---|
| Contribution per unit | £16 | £24 |
| Labour hours per unit | 1.5 | 2.5 |
| Contribution per labour hour | 10.67 | 9.60 |

## Task 2.5

Use the data from Task 2.4, and your estimate of fixed costs calculated in Task 2.2, to prepare a memo to the Managing Director outlining

(a) how many of each line of trousers should be produced and sold;

(b) your reasons for choosing this production plan; and

(c) the profit that will be earned by the trouser-producing venture in the new unit

in the two separate situations below:

1 if production capacity is unlimited

2 if production is limited by the availability of only 900 labour hours

# MEMO

**To:** Managing Director **Subject:**

**From:** **Date:**

# PRACTICE EXAM BASED ASSESSMENT 3 UNIT 6

## EASTLEY LTD

**These tasks were set by the AAT in December 2002 and have been amended to reflect the Revised Standards**

**Time allowed: 3 hours plus 15 minutes reading time**

# INSTRUCTIONS

This exam based assessment is in TWO sections.

You have to show competence in BOTH sections. You should therefore attempt and aim to complete EVERY task in EACH section.

You should spend about 90 minutes on each section.

Include all essential calculations within your answers where appropriate.

The original paper contained four blank pages for workings.

Both sections are based on Eastley Ltd.

# SECTION 1 (Suggested time allowance: 90 minutes)

## DATA

Eastley Ltd manufactures ice cream. You work as an accounting technician at Eastley Ltd, reporting to the FInance Director.

The company manufactures a range of different flavoured ice creams, although its most popular product is a plain ice cream known as Pure Delight. All ice cream recipes include water, cream and sugar.

The Finance Director has given you the following tasks.

## Task 1.1

Complete the following stock card for sugar for November 2004 on a LIFO basis.

| STOCK CARD | | | | | | |
|---|---|---|---|---|---|---|
| **Product:** | **Sugar** | | | | | |
| | *Receipts* | | | *Issues* | *Balance* | |
| *Date* | *Quantity (kgs)* | *Cost per kg £* | *Total Cost £* | *Quantity (kgs)* | *Quantity (kgs)* | *Total Cost £* |
| B/f at 1 Nov | 50,000 | 1.00 | 50,000 | | 50,000 | 50,000 |
| 4 Nov | 20,000 | 1.20 | 24,000 | | 70,000 | 74,000 |
| 7 Nov | | | | 15,000 | | |
| 16 Nov | 35,000 | 0.90 | | | | |
| 19 Nov | | | | 20,000 | | |
| 24 Nov | | | | 25,000 | | |

# ADDITIONAL DATA

In the financial accounts, stock is valued using the FIFO method.

## Task 1.2

Use the data given in Task 1.1 to calculate the FIFO value of the stock of sugar at 30 November 2004.

..........

..........

..........

..........

..........

# ADDITIONAL DATA

Eastley Ltd has the following departments:

- Manufacturing
- Packing
- Stores
- Maintenance

The budgeted fixed overheads for December are as follows.

| | £ |
|---|---|
| Depreciation | 4,800 |
| Rent | 20,000 |
| Other property overheads | 8,000 |
| Maintenance costs | 15,200 |
| Staff costs: | |
| Indirect packing | 1,800 |
| Indirect manufacturing | 4,650 |
| Stores | 8,750 |
| Maintenance | 4,200 |
| Total budgeted fixed overheads | 67,400 |

The following information is also relevant.

| *Department* | *% of floor space occupied* | *Net book value of fixed assets* £000 | *Materials requisitions* | *Maintenance hours usage* |
|---|---|---|---|---|
| Manufacturing | 75% | 900 | 120 | 70% |
| Packing | 10% | 40 | 80 | 20% |
| Stores | 10% | 20 | – | 10% |
| Maintenance | 5% | 40 | – | – |
| | 100% | 1,000 | 200 | 100% |

Overheads are allocated and apportioned between departments using the most appropriate basis.

## Task 1.3

Complete the table below to show the basis for allocation and apportionment of budgeted fixed overheads between the four departments

| | *OVERHEAD ALLOCATION* | | | *APPORTIONMENT* | | |
|---|---|---|---|---|---|---|
| *Budgeted fixed overheads* for December 2002 | *Basis* | *Total* £ | *Manufacturing* £ | *Packing* £ | *Stores* £ | *Maintenance* £ |
| Depreciation | NBV | 4,800 | 4320 | 192 | 96 | 192 |
| Rent | FLOOR SPACE | 20,000 | 15,000 | 2,000 | 2,000 | 1,000 |
| Other property overheads | FLOOR SPACE. | 8,000 | 6,000 | 800 | 800 | 400 |
| Maintenance costs | ALLOCATED | 15,200 | | | | 15,200 |
| Staff costs | ALLOCATED | 19,400 | 4650 | 1800 | 8750 | 4200 |
| Total fixed overheads | | 67,400 | 29,970 | 4792 | 11,646 | 20,992 |
| **Reapportionment:** | | | | | | (20,992) |
| Maintenance | HOURS USED | | 14,694 | 4199 | 2099 | – |
| | | | 44,664 | 8991 | (13,745) | – |
| Stores | | | 8247 | 5498 | – | – |
| | | | 52911 | 14,489 | – | – |

## ADDITIONAL DATA

Overheads in the manufacturing department are absorbed into the cost of products on the basis of machine hours and the packing department overheads are absorbed on the basis of direct labour hours. Budgeted machine hours and direct labour hours for December 2004 are as follows:

| | **Machine hours** | **Direct labour hours** |
|---|---|---|
| Manufacturing | 2,100 | 1,400 |
| Packing | 300 | 1,200 |

$\frac{\text{TOTAL OVERHEADS}}{\text{HRS}}$

## Task 1.4

Calculate the overhead absorption rate in each department to two decimal places.

MANUFACTURING – $\frac{52,911}{2100}$ = £25.19 per hour.

PACKING – $\frac{14,489}{1,200}$ = £12.07 per hour.

## ADDITIONAL DATA

Given below are the production details of 100 litres of three of Eastley Ltd's main products:

| | | Manufacturing | Packing |
|---|---|---|---|
| Jasmine Pearl | – machine hours | 3 | 0.5 |
| | labour hours | 2 | 1.0 |
| King Pin | – machine hours | 4.5 | 1.0 |
| | labour hours | 3 | 1.5 |
| Lolly Desert | – machine hours | 2.5 | 0.2 |
| | labour hours | 1.5 | 2.0 |

### Task 1.5

Calculate the total amount of overhead to be included in the cost of 100 litres of each of these products.

## ADDITIONAL DATA

The production director has commented that the allocation and apportionment of the overheads appears fairly arbitrary.

### Task 1.6

You are to write a report to the production director on the blank report overleaf explaining the following:

- how total absorption costing works and its benefits despite its arbitrary nature
- the alternative approach of marginal costing and its benefits
- a comparison of the two methods for both costing and reporting purposes (include in this the different effects on profit of the two methods if stock levels are changing)

REPORT

To: FINANCE DIRECTOR

From: AT

Subject: ABSORPTION COSTING

Date:

Absorption costing is a way of costing that includes all costs in the final production cost.

Marginal costing costs everything except the fixed costs. They are accounted for after the production cost has been worked out.

Absorption costing does include all costs but for decision making, marginal costing may be better.

## ADDITIONAL DATA

The Finance Director wishes you to calculate the budgeted cost for January 2005 of 1,000 litres of Pure Delight. To do this you are given the following information.

- Monthly manufacturing fixed costs £12,500
- Unit variable costs per 1,000 litres of production £600

You are also told that the production volume in January 2003 will be either 100,000 litres or 125,000 litres.

### Task 1.7

Complete the table below to show, for both possible production volumes:

a) the total cost of production;

b) the cost per 1,000 litres.

| *Product: Pure Delight* | *Production* | |
|---|---|---|
| Production volume | 100,000 litres<br>£ | 125,000 litres<br>£ |
| Fixed costs | 12500 | 12500 |
| Variable costs | 60000 | 75000 |
| Total costs | 72500 | 87500 |
| Cost per 1,000 litres | 72500 | 87500 |
| | | |

# SECTION 2 (Suggested time allowance: 90 minutes)

## DATA

Eastley Ltd is considering opening a new division which will produce a single range of ice creams and the Finance Director has asked for your help in a number of matters.

The Finance Director had determined sales income and production costs at a monthly production level of 300,000 litres and 400,000 litres. These are given below.

| | *Production level* | |
|---|---|---|
| | *300,000 litres* | *400,000 litres* |
| | £ | £ |
| Sales income | 540,000 | 720,000 |
| Manufacturing costs | 210,000 | 280,000 |
| Packing costs | 90,000 | 120,000 |
| Property costs | 110,000 | 110,000 |
| Maintenance costs | 84,000 | 102,000 |
| Total costs | 494,000 | 612,000 |
| Profit | 46,000 | 108,000 |

The Finance Director has informed you that he thinks that in fact, in the early days of the division, production will be 320,000 litres.

### Task 2.1

Provide the Finance Director with a forecast of income and costs, based upon the cost predictions above, for a production and sales level of 320,000 litres per month.

### Task 2.2

The Finance Director has also asked you to calculate the following figures.

a) the breakeven sales in litres

..........................................................................................................

..........................................................................................................

..........................................................................................................

..........................................................................................................

..........................................................................................................

..........................................................................................................

b) assuming that expected sales are 320,000 litres each month, the margin of safety

..............................................................................................................

..............................................................................................................

..............................................................................................................

..............................................................................................................

..............................................................................................................

..............................................................................................................

c) the level of sales that will produce a monthly profit of £100,000

..............................................................................................................

..............................................................................................................

..............................................................................................................

..............................................................................................................

..............................................................................................................

..............................................................................................................

## ADDITIONAL DATA

The Finance Director has discovered that if production levels reach 360,000 litres per month then a bulk discount can be negotiated on supplies of materials reducing the manufacturing cost by 10%.

### Task 2.3

Calculate the profit to be made at this level of sales and production after altering the manufacturing cost for the bulk discount.

..............................................................................................................

..............................................................................................................

..............................................................................................................

..............................................................................................................

..............................................................................................................

..............................................................................................................

..............................................................................................................

..............................................................................................................

..............................................................................................................

..............................................................................................................

..............................................................................................................

..............................................................................................................

..............................................................................................................

# ADDITIONAL DATA

It is planned that the new division will use some surplus machinery from one of the other factories for the next five years. However, the production manager has estimated that if new machinery is purchased, at a cost of £500,000, annual savings in manufacturing costs over the use costs of using the existing machinery can be made as follows:

664,010.

| | | |
|---|---|---|
| Year 1 | £180,000 | 180,000 |
| Year 2 | £150,000 | 330,000 |
| Year 3 | £120,000 | 450,000 |
| Year 4 | £100,000 | 550,000 |
| Year 5 | £80,000 | 630,000 |

35950

The company's cost of capital is 8% and the discount factors at this rate are given below:

| Year | Discount factor | |
|---|---|---|
| 1 | 0.926 | 166,680 |
| 2 | 0.857 | 128,550 |
| 3 | 0.794 | 95,280 |
| 4 | 0.735 | 73,500 |
| 5 | 0.681 | 54,480 |
| | | 518,490 |

£18,490

## Task 2.4

a) Calculate the payback period of the new machinery

3yrs + (50,000/100,000 x12) - 6mths

b) Calculate the net present value of the machinery investment at the company's cost of capital.

£18,490.

c) Write a memo to the Finance Director, using the sheet of memo paper overleaf, informing him of the results of the calculations made in this task, stating any assumptions made in the calculations and concluding as to whether this proposed investment is financially worthwhile.

## MEMO

To: FINANCE DIRECTOR.

From:

Subject:

Date:

---

Please see attached my results.
As you can see, the machine has a positive net present value + is therefore worth undertaking.

**Task 2.5**

Briefly explain what is meant by a positive net present value.

It means that you have a good return + It's worth doing.

**Task 2.6**

What is the internal rate of return of a project? You are not required to perform any calculations.

It's the net present value that gives you zero.

# PRACTICE EXAM BASED ASSESSMENT 4 UNIT 6

## GIFT LTD

**This is the AAT's specimen exam based assessment**

**Time allowed: 3 hours plus 15 minutes reading time**

This examination paper is in TWO sections.

You have to show competence in BOTH sections.

You should therefore attempt and aim to complete EVERY task in BOTH sections.

All essential workings should be included within your answers, where appropriate.

You should spend about 90 minutes on each section.

Both sections are based on Gift Ltd.

# SECTION 1 (Suggested time allowance: 90 minutes)

## DATA

Gift Ltd manufactures and sells toys. You work as an accounting technician at Gift Ltd, reporting to the Finance Director.

All toys are manufactured using plastic. The biggest selling item is Meg, a toy doll made from pink plastic. The company operates an integrated absorption costing system. Stocks are valued on a first in first out basis.

The Finance Director has given you the following tasks:

### Task 1.1

Complete the following stock card for pink plastic using the FIFO method for valuing issues to production and stocks of materials.

**STOCK CARD**

**Product:** **Pink plastic**

| | *Receipts* | | | *Issues* | | | *Balance* | |
|---|---|---|---|---|---|---|---|---|
| *Date* | *Quantity kgs* | *Cost per kg* | *Total Cost* | *Quantity kgs* | *Cost per kg* | *Total Cost* | *Quantity kgs* | *Total Cost* |
| | | £ | £ | | £ | £ | | £ |
| B/f at 1.11.03 | | | | | | | 10,000 | 10,000 |
| 6.11.03 | 20,000 | 1.10 | 22,000 | | | | 30,000 | 32,000 |
| 11.11.03 | | | | 16,000 | | | | |
| 17.11.03 | 10,000 | 1.20 | 12,000 | | | | | |
| 19.11.03 | | | | 20,000 | | | | |

## ADDITIONAL DATA

All issues of pink plastic are for the manufacture of Meg dolls. The following cost accounting codes are used to record material costs:

| *Code number* | *Description* |
|---|---|
| 1000 | Stock of pink plastic |
| 1100 | Work in progress – Meg dolls |
| 3000 | Creditors control |

### Task 1.2

Complete the table below to record separately the two purchases and two issues of pink plastic in the cost accounting records.

| Date | Code | Dr | Cr |
|---|---|---|---|
| 6 Nov | 1000 | | |
| 6 Nov | 3000 | | |
| 11 Nov | 1000 | | |
| 11 Nov | 1100 | | |
| 17 Nov | 1000 | | |
| 17 Nov | 3000 | | |
| 19 Nov | 1000 | | |
| 19 Nov | 1100 | | |

## ADDITIONAL DATA

Direct labour overtime payments are included in direct costs. The following data relates to the production of Meg dolls for November:

| | |
|---|---|
| Total direct labour hours worked | 12,000 hours |
| Normal time hours | 10,600 hours |
| Overtime hours | 1,400 hours |
| Normal time rate per hour | £6 per hour |
| Overtime premium per hour | £3 per hour |

## Task 1.3

Calculate the total cost of direct labour for November.

..........................................................................................................................................

..........................................................................................................................................

..........................................................................................................................................

..........................................................................................................................................

..........................................................................................................................................

..........................................................................................................................................

..........................................................................................................................................

..........................................................................................................................................

## ADDITIONAL DATA

Gift Ltd has the following departments:

- Warehouse
- Manufacturing
- Sales
- Accounting

The budgeted and actual fixed overheads of the company for November were as follows:

| | £ |
|---|---|
| Depreciation | 7,400 |
| Rent | 2,500 |
| Other property overheads | 3,200 |
| Accounting overheads | 6,250 |
| Staff costs: | |
| Warehouse | 4,230 |
| Indirect manufacturing | 3,015 |
| Sales | 6,520 |
| Accounting | 5,160 |
| Total budgeted and actual fixed overheads | 38,275 |

The following information is also relevant:

| *Department* | *% of floor space occupied* | *Net book value of fixed assets* |
|---|---|---|
| | | £000 |
| Warehouse | 15% | 180 |
| Manufacturing | 70% | 540 |
| Sales | 10% | - |
| Accounting | 5% | 80 |
| | 100% | 800 |

Overheads are allocated and apportioned between departments using the most appropriate basis.

## Task 1.4

Complete the following table showing the allocation and apportionment of fixed overheads between the four departments.

| *Fixed overheads for November* | *Basis* | *Total* £ | *Warehouse* £ | *Manufacturing* £ | *Sales* £ | *Accounting* £ |
|---|---|---|---|---|---|---|
| Depreciation | | 7,400 | | | | |
| Rent | | 2,500 | | | | |
| Other property overheads | | 3,200 | | | | |
| Accounting overheads | | 6,250 | | | | |
| Staff costs | | 18,825 | | | | |
| | | 33,275 | | | | |

## ADDITIONAL DATA

Manufacturing fixed overheads are absorbed on the basis of budgeted direct labour hours. The following information relates to the manufacturing department for November:

- The budgeted number of direct labour hours was 20,000 hours.
- The actual direct labour hours worked producing Meg dolls were 12,000 hours.
- 36,000 Meg dolls were produced with a material cost for pink plastic of £39,200.

## Task 1.5

Use the data from task 1.4 to calculate the budgeted fixed overhead absorption rate for the manufacturing department for November.

..........................................................................................................................................................

..........................................................................................................................................................

..........................................................................................................................................................

..........................................................................................................................................................

..........................................................................................................................................................

..........................................................................................................................................................

## Task 1.6

Use the information from tasks 1.3 and 1.5 to complete the table below to show:

a) the total cost of production;
b) the unit cost of production of a Meg doll for November.

| Product: Meg Doll | £ |
|---|---|
| Direct costs | |
| Pink plastic | |
| Direct labour | |
| Indirect costs | |
| Manufacturing department overheads | |
| Total cost of production | |
| Unit cost of production (to the nearest penny) | |

# SECTION 2 (Suggested time allowance: 90 minutes)

## DATA

In addition to producing Meg dolls, the company manufactures and sells three types of doll house, products E, C and R. The expected monthly costs and sales information for each product is as follows:

| Product | E | C | R |
|---|---|---|---|
| Sales and production units | 2,000 | 1,500 | 500 |
| Machine hours per month | 200 | 225 | 175 |
| Total sales revenue | £60,000 | £60,000 | £30,000 |
| Total direct materials | £20,000 | £16,500 | £6,000 |
| Total direct labour | £32,000 | £24,000 | £10,000 |
| Total variable overheads | £4,000 | £2,625 | £3,500 |

The total expected monthly fixed costs relating to the production of all doll houses are £4,800.

### Task 2.1

Complete the table below to show for each product the expected contribution per unit.

| Product | E<br>£ | C<br>£ | R<br>£ |
|---|---|---|---|
| Selling price per unit | | | |
| Less: Unit variable costs | | | |
| Direct materials | | | |
| Direct labour | | | |
| Variable overheads | | | |
| Contribution per unit | | | |

## Task 2.2

If the company only manufactures product E, calculate the number of units it would need to make and sell each month to cover the fixed costs of £4,800.

........................................................................................................................................................

........................................................................................................................................................

........................................................................................................................................................

........................................................................................................................................................

........................................................................................................................................................

## ADDITIONAL DATA

The breakdown of a machine used in the manufacture of doll houses has reduced available machine time from 600 to 365 hours. The Finance Director asks you to calculate the contribution of each doll house per machine hour.

## Task 2.3

Use the data from task 2.1 to complete the table below.

| Product | E | C | R |
|---|---|---|---|
| Contribution per unit | | | |
| Machine hours per unit | | | |
| Contribution per machine hour | | | |

## Task 2.4

Use the data from task 2.3 to calculate how many units of products E, C and R the company should make and sell to maximize its profits using 365 machine hours.

## ADDITIONAL DATA

The company requires an annual rate of return of 10% on any new project. The Managing Director has asked you to appraise the financial effects of introducing a new doll house. You are given the following information relating to this product:

| | Year 1 | Year 2 | Year 3 | Year 4 | Year 5 |
|---|---|---|---|---|---|
| | £000 | £000 | £000 | £000 | £000 |
| Design costs | 80 | | | | |
| Sales revenues | | 30 | 50 | 160 | 50 |
| Variable costs | | 15 | 25 | 80 | 25 |
| 10% Present value factor | 0.909 | 0.826 | 0.751 | 0.683 | 0.621 |

### Task 2.5

Calculate for the new doll house project:

a) the payback period

..........................................................................................................................

..........................................................................................................................

..........................................................................................................................

..........................................................................................................................

b) the net present value

..........................................................................................................................

..........................................................................................................................

..........................................................................................................................

..........................................................................................................................

### Task 2.6

Use the data from task 2.5 to prepare a report to the Managing Director on the new doll house project. Your report should:

a) identify TWO additional items of information relevant to appraising this project,

b) recommend whether to accept or reject the project based on its net present value.

# REPORT

**To:** **From:** **Date:**

# AAT

## SAMPLE SIMULATION
## UNIT 6

# QUALITY CANDLES LTD

This is the AAT's Sample Simulation for Unit 6. Its purpose is to give you an idea of what an AAT simulation looks like. It is not intended as a definitive guide to the tasks you may be required to perform.

The suggested time allowance for this Assessment is four hours. Up to 30 minutes extra time may be permitted in an AAT simulation. Breaks in assessment may be allowed in the AAT simulation, but it must normally be completed in one day.

Calculators may be used but no reference material is permitted.

# COVERAGE OF PERFORMANCE CRITERIA AND RANGE STATEMENTS

**All performance criteria are covered in this simulation.**

| Element | PC Coverage |
|---|---|
| **6.1** | **Record and analyse information relating to direct costs and revenues** |
| (a) | Identify direct costs in accordance with the organisation's costing procedures. |
| (b) | Record and analyse information relating to direct costs. |
| (c) | Calculate direct costs in accordance with the organisation's policies and procedures. |
| (d) | Check cost information for stock against usage and stock control practices. |
| (e) | Resolve or refer queries to the appropriate person. |
| **6.2** | **Record and analyse information relating to the allocation, apportionment and absorption of overhead costs** |
| (a) | Identify overhead costs in accordance with the organisation's procedures. |
| (b) | Attribute overhead costs to production and service cost centres in accordance with agreed bases of allocation and apportionment. |
| (c) | Calculate overhead absorption rates in accordance with agreed bases of absorption. |
| (d) | Record and analyse information relating to overhead costs in accordance with the organisation's procedures. |
| (e) | Make adjustments for under and over recovered overhead costs in accordance with established procedures. |
| (f) | Review methods of allocation, apportionment and absorption at regular intervals in discussions with senior staff, and ensure agreed changes to methods are implemented. |
| (g) | Consult staff working in operational departments to resolve any queries in overhead cost data. |
| **6.3** | **Prepare and evaluate estimates of costs and revenues** |
| (a) | Identify information relevant to estimating current and future revenues and costs. |
| (b) | Prepare estimates of future income and costs. |
| (c) | Calculate the effects of variations in capacity on product costs. |
| (d) | Analyse critical factors affecting costs and revenues using appropriate accounting techniques and draw clear conclusions from the analysis. |
| (e) | State any assumptions used when evaluating future costs and revenues. |
| (f) | Identify and evaluate options and solutions for their contribution to organisational goals. |
| (g) | Present recommendations to appropriate people in a clear and concise way and supported by a clear rationale. |

**Any missing range statements should be assessed separately.**

# PART ONE

## INSTRUCTIONS

This simulation is designed to let you show your ability to record and evaluate costs and revenues.

The simulation is designed to be attempted in two parts. You are allowed four hours in total to complete your work. You should spend:

- two hours on the tasks in Part 1, covering Elements 6.1 and 6.2;
- two hours on the tasks in Part 2, covering Element 6.3.

The simulation contains a large volume of data which you will need in order to complete the tasks. The information you require is provided in the sequence in which you will need to deal with it. However you are advised to look quickly through all of the material before you begin. This will help you to familiarise yourself with the situation and the information available.

Write your answers in the answer booklet provided on pages 139 to 157. If you need more paper for your answers, ask the person in charge.

You should write your answers in blue or black ink, not pencil. You may use correcting fluid, but in moderation. You should cross out your errors neatly and clearly.

Your work must be accurate, so check your work carefully before handing it in.

**Coverage of performance criteria and range statements**

It is not always possible to cover all performance criteria and range statements in a single simulation. Any performance criteria and range statements not covered must be assessed by other means by the assessor before a candidate can be considered competent.

Performance criteria and range statement coverage for this simulation is shown on page 120.

# THE SITUATION

Your name is Bobby Forster and you work as the Accounts Assistant for Quality Candles Limited. The company manufactures candles of all kinds, including hand made candles. The candles are sold to wholesalers, to retailers, and direct to the public through the company's mail order division.

**The manufacturing operations**

The manufacturing operations involve three production cost centres and two service cost centres.

| *Production cost centres* | *Service cost centres* |
|---|---|
| Manufacturing | Stores |
| Painting and finishing | Maintenance |
| Packing | |

**The time period covered by this simulation**

The company's year end is 31 December. This simulation is concerned with activities during the quarter ending 31 December 2003, and with planning activities for the year ending 31 December 2004.

# THE TASKS TO BE COMPLETED (PART ONE)

**Element 6.1 (one hour)**

1. Refer to the stores record card on page 139 of the answer booklet.

   - Complete this stores record card using the information from the materials documentation on page 140 of the answer booklet and page 126 of this book. You will need to identify and apply the stock valuation method in use and you are advised that VAT is not entered in the cost accounting records.

   - Show the volume and value of the stock at the close of the week ending 10 October 2003. Any returns from production cost centres to stores are valued at the price of the most recent batch issued from stores.

2. Refer to the materials requisition note and materials returned note on page 140 of the answer booklet.

   - Complete the column headed 'Cost office use only' on each of the two documents.

3. Refer to your completed stores record card on page 139 of the answer booklet.

   - Prepare a memo for the general manager, drawing attention to any unusual issues concerning the stock levels for this item during the week. Your memo should highlight the issues, point out any possible consequences, and suggest any action that might be taken to prevent the unusual situations occurring. Use the blank memo form on page 141 of the answer booklet.

4. Refer to the internal policy document on page 126 of this book and the piecework operation card on page 142 of the answer booklet.

   - Complete the piecework operation card using the information provided. You will need to do the following:

     - Calculate the piecework payment for each day.
     - Calculate any bonus payable for the day.
     - Calculate the total wages payable for the day.
     - Complete the analysis of total wages payable for the week.

5. Refer to the piecework operation card on page 142 of the answer booklet.

   - Identify any possible discrepancy in the activity data and write a memo to the supervisor, Roy Hart, explaining clearly what you think the discrepancy might be. Use the blank memo form on page 143 of the answer booklet.

**Element 6.2 (one hour)**

**6.** Refer to the memo on page 127 of this book.

- Perform the production overhead allocation and apportionment exercise using the analysis sheet on page 144 of the answer booklet. You will see that the task has already been started in respect of indirect labour. The data that you have gathered is on pages 127 and 128 of this booklet.

7. Refer to the first memo on page 129 of this book.

- Calculate the production overhead absorption rates for 2004. You will need to make use of the following:

  - The blank working paper on page 145 of the answer booklet;
  - The data on pages 127 and 128 of this booklet;
  - Your results for the total production department overhead for 2004 on page 144 of the answer booklet.

  All absorption rates should be calculated to the nearest penny.

**8.** Refer to the second memo on page 129 of this book.

- Re-calculate the total production overhead for each production department, reversing the order of apportionment of the service department overheads. Use the working paper on page 146 of the answer booklet. You will need to do the following:

  - Transfer your figures for total department overhead for all five departments from your overhead analysis sheet on page 144 of the answer booklet.
  - Re-apportion the service department overheads, apportioning the stores costs first to the other four departments on the basis of the number of material requisitions. Then re-apportion the total overhead of the maintenance department to the three production departments, on the basis of maintenance hours.

Perform all calculations to the nearest £000.

**9** ■ Review your results from task 8 and write a memo to the general manager. In your memo you should:

  - comment on the effect of the change in method;
  - explain whether you think it is necessary to instigate a change in the method of re-apportionment of service department costs.

  Use the blank memo form on page 147 of the answer booklet.

**10.** Refer to the memo and the production overhead data on page 130 of this book.

- Complete the journal entry form on page 148 of the answer booklet.
- Write a memo to the production manager detailing any queries concerning the data and suggesting possible causes of any discrepancies you have identified. Use the blank memo form on page 149 of the answer booklet.

# SALES INVOICE

**Threadshop Limited**
25 Lyme Street, Taunton TA2 4RP

Invoice to:
Quality Candles Limited
2 Norman Lane
Winterbury
RT5 8UT

| | |
|---|---|
| VAT Registration: | 254 1781 26 |
| Date/tax point: | 9 October 2003 |
| Invoice numvber: | T543 |
| Your order: | 47346 |

| Description of goods/services | Total (£) |
|---|---|
| Candlewick thread, 200 metre rolls<br>80 rolls @ £2.38 | 190.40 |
| Goods total<br>VAT @ 17.5% | 190.40<br>33.32 |
| Total due | 223.72 |

| | |
|---|---|
| Checked against GRN number: | 427 |
| Date received: | 9 October 2003 |
| Signed: | J Jones |

Terms: net 30 days

# INTERNAL POLICY DOCUMENT

**Document no:** 18
**Subject:** Wages
**Issued:** August 2003

---

**Piecework scheme**

A piecework scheme is to be introduced into the manufacturing department in order to reward efficient and productive operatives.

A piecework rate per batch of £0.50 will be paid for each batch of accepted output produced during a day.

In addition a bonus will be paid of 4 per cent of the piecework payment for any day on which the number of batches rejected by Quality Control is less than 5 per cent of the total number of batches produced.

A guaranteed daily wage of £50 is payable if the piecework payment + bonus amounts to less than £50 in any day.

**Analysis of wages**

Piecework payments and guaranteed daily wages paid will be treated as direct wages costs.

Bonus payments will be treated as indirect wages costs.

**Discrepancies on piecework operation cards**

The company wishes to pay wages and report labour rates promptly. Therefore employees will initially be paid for the total wages calculated according to the data contained on the weekly piecework operation card.

Any discrepancies on operation cards will be referred to the supervisor. Any alterations to wages will be agreed with the employee before adjustment is made to the next wage payment.

## INTERNAL MEMO

**To:** Bobby Forster, Accounts Assistant
**From:** General Manager
**Subject:** Budgeted production costs for 2004
**Date:** 28 October 2003

---

As you know we have begun our budgetary planning exercise for 2004.

I understand that you have been working on the analysis of budgeted production costs. Could you please pull together all the information you have gathered and carry out the allocation and apportionment exercise for production overhead costs for 2004.

Thanks. Then we will have the necessary information that we need to calculate the pre-determined overhead absorption rates for 2004.

**Data for production overhead analysis for 2004**

**1. Summary of budgeted production costs for 2004**

| | £000 |
|---|---:|
| Direct materials | 200 |
| Indirect materials | 40 |
| Direct labour | 420 |
| Indirect labour: | |
| Manufacturing department | 22 |
| Painting and finishing department | 14 |
| Packing department | 11 |
| Stores | 35 |
| Maintenance | 16 |
| Rent and rates | 105 |
| Protective clothing | 31 |
| Power | 40 |
| Insurance | 24 |
| Heat and light | 35 |
| Depreciation | 48 |
| Other production overheads | 15 |
| Total budgeted production costs | 1,056 |

## 2. Other data

| | *Manufacturing* | *Painting/ finishing* | *Packing* | *Stores* | *Maintenance* |
|---|---|---|---|---|---|
| Direct materials cost (£000) | 150 | 25 | 25 | - | - |
| Floor area (000 sq metres) | 30 | 10 | 16 | 8 | 6 |
| Power usage (%) | 50 | 10 | 30 | 5 | 5 |
| Net book value of equipment (£000) | 220 | 80 | 120 | 40 | 20 |
| Maintenance hours (000) | 7 | 4 | 3 | 1 | - |
| Materials requisitions (000) | 18 | 10 | 9 | - | 11 |
| Direct labour hours (000) | 20 | 28 | 10 | - | - |
| Machine hours (000) | 200 | 14 | 90 | - | - |

## 3. Company procedures for the allocation and apportionment of production overheads

- 30 per cent of the total indirect materials cost is apportioned to stores and 30 per cent to maintenance. The remaining 40 per cent is apportioned to the production departments according to the direct materials cost.
- Rent and rates and heating and lighting costs are apportioned according to the floor area occupied by each department.
- The cost of protective clothing is allocated to the manufacturing department.
- Power costs are apportioned according to the power usage in each department.
- Insurance and depreciation costs are apportioned according to the net book value of equipment in each department.
- Other production overheads are apportioned equally to the production departments.
- The total cost of the maintenance department is apportioned to the other four departments according to the number of maintenance hours.
- After a charge has been received from the maintenance department, the total cost of the stores department is apportioned to the three production departments according to the number of material requisitions.
- All calculations are rounded to the nearest £000.

## INTERNAL MEMO

**To:** Bobby Forster, Accounts Assistant
**From:** General Manager
**Subject:** Pre-determined overhead absorption rates
**Date:** 28 October 2003

---

Many thanks for all your hard work on the overhead analysis.

Could you please now use the results of your analysis to calculate overhead absorption rates for the three production departments for 2004. We have decided that the most appropriate bases of absorption will be as follows:

- Manufacturing department: machine hour rate;
- Painting and finishing department: labour hour rate;
- Packing department: machine hour rate.

Thanks for your help.

## INTERNAL MEMO

**To:** Bobby Forster, Accounts Assistant
**From:** General Manager
**Subject:** Re-apportionment of service department costs
**Date:** 4 November 2003

---

I have been giving some thought to the method that we use to re-apportion the service department costs to the production departments.

As you know, at present it is our policy to apportion the maintenance costs to all cost centres before we re-apportion the total stores costs to the production cost centres.

I would like to see the effect of altering the order of re-apportionment of service department costs. Could you please rework the figures so that we can review the results?

Let me have the results and your views as soon as possible, please.

## INTERNAL MEMO

**To:** Bobby Forster, Accounts Assistant
**From:** General Manager
**Subject:** Overhead absorption for October 2003
**Date:** 8 November 2003

---

As you know it is company policy to accumulate the under or over-absorbed production overhead each month in an account maintained for this purpose.

The production overhead data for October 2003 has now been finalised.

Could you please complete the journal entry for the absorption of production overhead into the work in progress accounts and transfer any under or over absorption for the month. Complete the entries using the data provided, but please let the production manager know if you have any queries concerning the data.

**Summary of production overhead data for October 2003**

| | £ |
|---|---|
| Actual production overhead incurred | 15,800 |
| Production overhead to be absorbed into work in progress | |
| Manufacturing department | 18,500 |
| Painting and finishing department | 7,400 |
| Packing department | 8,300 |

# PART TWO

## INSTRUCTIONS

This simulation is designed to let you show your ability to record and evaluate costs and revenues.

The simulation is designed to be attempted in two parts. You should already have completed the tasks in Part 1 and you should ensure that you have your answers to those tasks with you.

You are allowed four hours in total to complete your work.

- Two hours for the tasks in Part 1, covering Elements 6.1 and 6.2;
- Two hours for the tasks in Part 2, covering Element 6.3.

The simulation contains a large volume of data which you will need in order to complete the tasks. The information you require is provided in the sequence in which you will need to deal with it. However you are advised to look quickly through all of the material before you begin. This will help you to familiarise yourself with the situation and the information available.

Write your answers in the answer booklet provided on pages 139 to 157. If you need more paper for your answers, ask the person in charge.

You should write your answers in blue or black ink, not pencil.

You may use correcting fluid, but in moderation. You should cross out your errors neatly and clearly.

Your work must be accurate, so check your work carefully before handing it in.

# THE SITUATION

Your name is Bobby Forster and you work as the Accounts Assistant for Quality Candles Limited. The company manufactures candles of all kinds, including hand made candles. The candles are sold to wholesalers, to retailers, and direct to the public through the company's mail order division.

**The manufacturing operations**

The manufacturing operations involve three production cost centres and two service cost centres.

| *Production cost centres* | *Service cost centres* |
|---|---|
| Manufacturing | Stores |
| Painting and finishing | Maintenance |
| Packing | |

**The time period covered by this simulation**

The company's year end is 31 December. This simulation is concerned with activities during the quarter ending 31 December 2003, and with planning activities for the year ending 31 December 2004.

# THE TASKS TO BE COMPLETED (PART TWO)

**Element 6.3 (two hours)**

**11.** Refer to the memo on page 134 of this book and prepare the necessary information in response to the general manager's query. You will need to do the following.

- Use the data on page 134 of this book and the working paper on page 150 of the answer booklet to identify the cost and revenue behaviour patterns to be used in your projections.
- Use your identified cost and revenue behaviour patterns to complete the planned profit projection on page 151 of the answer booklet. There is space for your workings at the bottom of that page.

**12.** Refer to the first memo on page 135 of this book and answer the General Manager's queries. You will need to do the following.

(i) Use your identified cost and revenue behaviour patterns, adjusted for the change in materials cost, to prepare a revised planned profit statement for December. Complete the profit statement on page 152 of the answer booklet. There is space for your workings at the bottom of that page.

(ii) Calculate the breakeven point in terms of the number of cases to be sold in December if the bulk discount is accepted. Use the blank working paper on page 153 of the answer booklet and round your answer up to the nearest number of whole cases. Also use the same working paper to calculate the margin of safety. Express your answer as a percentage of the increased planned activity for December.

(iii) Prepare a memo to the general manager evaluating the results of your calculations. Your memo should contain the following:

- Your comments on the resulting profit, breakeven point and margin of safety;
- A statement of any assumptions you have used in evaluating the proposal.

Use the blank memo form on page 154 of the answer booklet.

**13.** Refer to the second memo on page 135 of this book and do the following:

(i) Use the working paper on page 155 of the answer booklet to calculate the payback period and the net present value of the proposed investment. Ignore inflation and perform all monetary calculations to the nearest £.

(ii) Write a memo to the General Manager evaluating the proposal from a financial viewpoint and stating any assumptions you have made in your analysis. Use the blank memo form on page 156 of the answer booklet.

# INTERNAL MEMO

**To:** Bobby Forster, Accounts Assistant
**From:** General Manager
**Subject:** Mail order division: revised plan for December 2003
**Date:** 9 November 2003

---

Could you please prepare the revised cost and revenue plan for the mail order division for December.

The plan is to sell 6,800 cases of candles and we will base our projections on the cost and revenue behaviour patterns experienced during August to October.

Thanks for your help.

**Quality Candles Limited: mail order division**

**Actual results for August to October 2003**

| | *August* | *September* | *October* |
|---|---|---|---|
| Number of cases sold | 7,000 | 6,200 | 5,900 |
| | £ | £ | £ |
| Candles cost | 9,100 | 8,060 | 7,670 |
| Packing materials cost | 5,250 | 4,650 | 4,425 |
| Packing labour cost | 2,100 | 1,860 | 1,770 |
| Packing overhead cost | 5,400 | 5,240 | 5,180 |
| Other overhead cost | 2,500 | *3,000 | 2,500 |
| Total costs | 24,350 | 22,810 | 21,545 |
| Sales revenue | 28,000 | 24,800 | 23,600 |
| Profit | 3,650 | 1,990 | 2,055 |

* Other overhead cost was £500 higher than usual during September owing to an unexpected machine breakdown which necessitated the hire of a packing machine to maintain production. This event will not recur in the future.

## INTERNAL MEMO

**To:** Bobby Forster, Accounts Assistant
**From:** General Manager
**Subject:** Mail order division: bulk discounts for December 2003
**Date:** 10 November 2003

---

Many thanks for your splendid work on the cost and revenue projections for December.

We are looking for opportunities to increase profit and we have just heard that we can obtain a bulk discount for packing materials in December if we increase our activity level to 7,600 cases for the month. This will mean that packing material unit costs will reduce by 20 per cent.

Could you please recalculate the profit projection for December if we decide to increase activity to take advantage of the discount.

Also, please calculate the breakeven point in terms of the number of cases to be sold in December if we make this change. I would also like to have a note of the margin of safety we will have.

Please let me have the results of your calculations and your comments on the outcome as soon as you can.

## INTERNAL MEMO

**To:** Bobby Forster, Accounts Assistant
**From:** General Manager
**Subject:** Purchase of delivery vehicles for mail order division
**Date:** 12 November 2003

---

We are considering the purchase and operation of our own fleet of delivery vehicles at the end of this year.

The distribution manager informs me that we will be able to cancel our current delivery contract and as a result we will enjoy cash savings of £34,800 each year from 2004 onwards, after taking account of the vehicle operating costs.

The vehicles will cost us £90,000 and will have a resale value of £5,000 when they are sold at the end of 2007.

Can you please appraise this proposal from a financial viewpoint? I need to know the payback period and the net present value at our usual discount rate of 12 per cent. As you know our minimum required payback period for all capital projects is three years.

Please let me have the results as soon as possible.

# ANSWER BOOKLET

# PART 1

## Task 1

### STORES RECORD CARD

Materials description: Candlewick thread, 200 metre rolls
Code no: CW728

Maximum quantity: 400
Minimum quantity: 140
Reorder level: 230
Reorder Quantity: 80

| | Receipts | | | | Issues | | | | Stock balance | | |
|---|---|---|---|---|---|---|---|---|---|---|---|
| Date 2003 | Document number | Qty | Price per roll (£) | Total (£) | Document number | Qty | Price per (£) | Total (£) | Qty | Price per roll (£) | Total (£) |
| 1 Oct | | | | | | | | | 28<br>26 | 2.20<br>2.30 | 61.60<br>59.80 |
| | | | | | | | | | 54 | | 121.40 |
| 3 Oct | | | | | 249 | 26<br>4 | 2.30<br>2.20 | 59.50<br>8.80 | | | |
| | | | | | | 30 | | 68.80 | 24 | 2.20 | 52.80 |
| 6 Oct | 419 | 80 | 235 | 188.00 | | | | | 24<br>80 | 2.20<br>2.35 | 52.80<br>188.00 |
| | | | | | | | | | 104 | | 240.80 |

## Task 2

### MATERIALS REQUISITION

Department: Manufacturing

Document no: 252

Date: 08/10/2003

| Code no | Description | Quantity | **Cost office use only** Value of issue (£) |
|---|---|---|---|
| CW728 | Candlewick thread 200m rolls | 40 | |

**Received by:** ..........................................  **Signature:** ..........................................

### MATERIALS RETURNED

Department: Manufacturing

Document no: 75

Date: 10/10/2003

| Code no | Description | Quantity | **Cost office use only** Value of issue(£) |
|---|---|---|---|
| CW728 | Candlewick thread 200m rolls | 3 | |

**Received by:** ..........................................  **Signature:** ..........................................

**Task 3**

## MEMO

**To:**
**From:**
**Subject:**
**Date:**

## Task 4

**QUALITY CANDLES LIMITED**
**PIECEWORK OPERATION CARD**

Operative name Mary Roberts Department: Manufacturing

Clock number R27

Week beginning 6 October 2003

| Activity | Monday | Tuesday | Wednesday | Thursday | Friday |
|---|---|---|---|---|---|
| Batches produced | 120 | 102 | 34 | 202 | 115 |
| Batches rejected | 5 | 7 | 4 | 11 | 5 |
| Batches accepted | | | | | |
| Rate per batch | £ 0.50 | £ 0.50 | £ 0.50 | £ 0.50 | £ 0.50 |
| Piecework payment | £ | £ | £ | £ | £ |
| Bonus payable | £ | £ | £ | £ | £ |
| **Total payable for day*** | £ | £ | £ | £ | £ |

**Total wages payable for week:**

| | £ |
|---|---|
| Direct wages | |
| Indirect wages | |
| Total wages | |

* Guaranteed daily wage of £50 is payable if piecework payment plus bonus amounts less than £50

Supervisor's signature: *A Peters*

**Task 5**

## INTERNAL MEMO

**To:**
**From:**
**Subject:**
**Date:**

## Task 6

**Production overhead analysis sheet for 2004**

| Production overhead item | Total £000 | Manufacturing £000 | Painting/ finishing £000 | Packing £000 | Stores £000 | Maintenance £000 |
|---|---|---|---|---|---|---|
| **Indirect labour** | 98 | 22 | 14 | 11 | 35 | 16 |
| | | | | | | |
| | | | | | | |
| | | | | | | |
| | | | | | | |
| | | | | | | |
| | | | | | | |
| | | | | | | |
| | | | | | | |
| | | | | | | |
| **Total department overheads** | | | | | | |
| **Apportion maintenance total** | – | | | | | ( ) |
| **Apportion stores total** | – | | | | ( ) | |
| **Total production dept overheads** | | | | | | |

## Task 7

**Working paper**

**Calculation of production overhead absorption rates for 2004**

---

*Manufacturing department*

---

*Painting and finishing department*

---

*Packing department*

## Task 8

**Sample calculations: working paper**
**Reversing the order of service department re-apportionments**

| Production overhead item | Total £000 | Manufacturing £000 | Painting/ finishing £000 | Packing £000 | Stores £000 | Maintenance £000 |
|---|---|---|---|---|---|---|
| **Total department overheads (from task 6)** | | | | | | |
| **Apportion stores total** | – | | | | ( ) | |
| **Apportion maintenance total** | – | | | | – | ( ) |
| **Total production dept overheads** | | | | | | |

**Task 9**

## INTERNAL MEMO

**To:**
**From:**
**Subject:**
**Date:**

## Task 10

**Journal entry for production overheads**

**October 2003**

*Entries for overhead absorbed during the month*

| | Debit (£) | Credit(£) |
|---|---|---|
| Work in progress: manufacture dept | | |
| Work in progress: painting and finishing dept | | |
| Work in progress: packing dept | | |
| Production overhead control | | |

*Entries for overhead under/over absorbed during this month*

| | Debit (£) | Credit(£) |
|---|---|---|
| Overhead over/under absorbed (P+L) | | |
| Production overhead control | | |

**Task 10 (continued)**

## INTERNAL MEMO

**To:**
**From:**
**Subject:**
**Date:**

# PART 2

## Task 11

**Workings for determination of revenue and cost behaviour patterns**

*Sales revenue*

*Candles cost*

*Packing materials cost*

*Packing labour cost*

*Packing overhead cost*

*Other overhead cost*

## Task 11 (continued)

**Quality Candles Limited: mail order division**

**Planned results for December 2003**

| | *December* |
|---|---|
| Number of cases to be sold | |
| | £ |
| Candles cost | |
| Packing materials cost | |
| Packing labour cost | |
| Packing overhead cost | |
| Other overhead cost | |
| Total costs | |
| Sales revenue | |
| Profit | |

**Space for workings**

## Task 12(i)

**Quality Candles Limited: mail order division**

**Planned results for December 2003: increased activity**

| | *December* |
|---|---|
| Number of cases to be sold | 7,600 |
| | £ |
| Candles cost | |
| Packing materials cost | |
| Packing labour cost | |
| Packing overhead cost | |
| Other overhead cost | |
| Total costs | |
| Sales revenue | |
| Profit | |

**Space for workings**

## Task 12 (ii)

**Quality Candles Limited: mail order division**

**Planned results for December 2003: increased activity**

*Calculation of breakeven point and margin of safety: working paper*

**Task 12 (iii)**

## INTERNAL MEMO

**To:**
**From:**
**Subject:**
**Date:**

## Task 13 (i)

**Working paper for the financial appraisal of purchase of delivery vehicles**

| Year | Cashflow £ | Discount factor @ 12% | Present value £ |
|---|---|---|---|
| 2003 | ____________ | 1.000 | ____________ |
| 2004 | ____________ | 0.893 | ____________ |
| 2005 | ____________ | 0.797 | ____________ |
| 2006 | ____________ | 0.712 | ____________ |
| 2007 | ____________ | 0.636 | ____________ |
| **Net present value** | | | ____________ |

**Working space for calculation of payback period**

**Task 13 (ii)**

## INTERNAL MEMO

**To:**
**From:**
**Subject:**
**Date:**

**If using this page, please state clearly which task you are answering.**

# AAT SAMPLE SIMULATION
# UNIT 7

## HOMER LTD

SIMULATION

# COVERAGE OF PERFORMANCE CRITERIA AND RANGE STATEMENTS

All performance criteria are covered in this simulation.

| Element | PC Coverage |
|---|---|
| **7.1** | **Prepare and present periodic performance reports** |
| (a) | Consolidate **information** derived from different units of the organisation into the appropriate form. |
| (b) | Reconcile **information** derived from different information systems within the organisation. |
| (c) | Compare results over time using an appropriate method that allows for changing price levels. |
| (d) | Account for transactions between separate units of the organisation in accordance with the organisation's procedures. |
| (e) | Calculate **ratios** and **performance indicators** in accordance with the organisation's procedures. |
| (f) | Prepare reports in the appropriate form and present them to management within the required timescales. |
| **7.2** | **Prepare reports and returns for outside agencies** |
| (a) | Identify, collate and present relevant information in accordance with the conventions and definitions used by outside agencies. |
| (b) | Ensure calculations of **ratios** and performance indicators are accurate. |
| (c) | Obtain authorisation for the despatch of completed **reports and returns** from the appropriate person. |
| (d) | Present **reports and returns** in accordance with outside agencies' requirements and deadlines. |
| **7.3** | **Prepare VAT returns** |
| (a) | Complete and submit VAT returns correctly, using data from the appropriate **recording systems**, within the statutory time limits. |
| (b) | Correctly identify and calculate relevant **inputs and outputs**. |
| (c) | Ensure submissions are made in accordance with current legislation. |
| (d) | Ensure guidance is sought from the VAT office when required, in a professional manner. |

Any missing range statements should be assessed separately.

# INSTRUCTIONS

This simulation is designed to let you show your ability to prepare reports and returns.

**You should read the whole simulation before you start work, so that you are fully aware of what you will have to do.**

You are allowed **three hours** to complete your work.

Write your answers in the answer booklet provided on pages 171 to 179. If you need more paper for your answers, ask the person in charge.

You should write your answers in blue or black ink, **not** pencil.

You may use correcting fluid, but in moderation. You should cross out your errors neatly and clearly.

Your work must be accurate, so check your work carefully before handing it in.

**Coverage of performance criteria and range statements**

It is not always possible to cover all performance criteria and range statements in a single simulation. Any performance criteria and range statements not covered must be assessed by other means by the assessor before a candidate can be considered competent.

Performance criteria and range statement coverage for this simulation is shown on page 160.

# THE SITUATION

Your name is Amir Pindhi and you work as an Accounts Assistant for Homer Limited, Sestos Drive, Pantile Trading Estate CV32 1AW.

Homer Limited is a manufacturing company, producing a single product, the 'Bart'. The company's year end is 31 March.

Today's date is Monday 14 April 2003.

**Divisional structure of Homer Limited**

All production activities are carried out in the Manufacturing division. This division transfers most of its output to the Sales Division, which sells the output to external customers.

The Manufacturing Division transfers finished output to the Sales division at full production cost, but without any mark-up for profit. The Manufacturing division also sells some of its finished output direct to external customers.

**Accounting for VAT**

Homer Limited is registered for VAT.

Sales of Barts to UK customers are subject to VAT at the standard rate of 17.5%.

The company also exports to other countries within the European Union (EU). Such exports qualify as zero-rated. The company does not export to countries outside the EU. The company does not import any goods or services.

The local VAT office for Homer Limited is at Bell House, 33 Lambert Road, Coventry CV12 8TR.

**Application for bank loan**

The company is about to seek a long-term loan from its bankers to finance expansion plans.

The bank has requested some financial information in support of this application, and one of your responsibilities will be to present this information in the form required by the bank.

**Presenting your work**

Unless you are told otherwise:

- all ratios and statistics should be computed and presented to two decimal places;
- monetary amounts should be computed and presented to the nearest penny.

# THE TASKS TO BE COMPLETED

**1.** Refer to the table on page 165 of this book which analyses monthly sales achieved by each of the company's two divisions during the years ended 31 March 2002 and 31 March 2003.

- Consolidate these figures to arrive at the monthly sales and cumulative sales for each month in the two year period. Note that this task relates only to sales made to external customers, not to transfers within the company from the Manufacturing division to the Sales division. You should set out your answer on the schedule on page 171 of the answer booklet.

**2.** Using the figures calculated in Task 1, plot a line graph on page 172 of the answer booklet. The graph should show the cumulative sales achieved month by month during the year ended 31 March 2002 and, as a separate line, the cumulative sales achieved month by month during the year ended 31 March 2003. As in Task 1, you are concerned only with the sales to external customers, not with internal transfers from Manufacturing to Sales.

**3.** On page 166 of this book you will find month-by-month values of an index appropriate to the industry in which Homer operates. The values given are stated by reference to a base figure of 100, which was the value of the index in the base period January 1998.

- Calculate the indexed value of the monthly sales to external customers, in March 2003 terms, for each month's sales in the year ended 31 March 2003. Your answer should be set out on page 173 of the answer booklet in accordance with the notes on that page.

**4.** Refer to the information on page 166 of this book.

- Complete the loan application form on page 174 of the answer booklet.
- Write a memo to the Accountant, Sonia Liesl, enclosing the form for her attention and approval prior to its submission to the bank. Use the blank memo form on page 175 of the answer booklet and date your memo 14 April 2003.

**5.** Write a memo to Sonia Liesl, presenting the following statistics for her information, and very briefly suggesting a possible reason for the movement in each statistic's value since year ended 31 March 2002. (The 2002 values are given in brackets below.)

- The gross profit percentage for year ended 31 March 2003 (The percentage in year ended 31 March 2002 was 43.15%).
- The net profit percentage for year ended 31 March 2003 (2002: 7.84%).
- The production cost per 'Bart' produced and sold in year ended 31 March 2003 (2002: £10.83).
- The value of sales earned per employee in year ended 31 March 2003 (2002: £26,018.13).

Use the memo form on page 176 of the answer booklet and date your memo 14 April 2003.

**6.** Refer to the information on pages 166 and 167 of this book that relates to the company's VAT return for the quarter ended on 31 March 2003.

- Complete the blank return on page 177 of the answer booklet. Note that the return is to be signed by the Accountant, Sonia Liesl, and that payment of any balance due to Customs & Excise will be made by cheque.

**7.** Refer to the memo from Sonia Liesl on page 167 of this booklet.

- Draft a letter to your local VAT office (in the name of Sonia Liesl) asking for the required information. Use the letterhead on page 178 of the answer booklet.

**8.** Reply to Sonia Liesl's memo giving her the brief details she requests, and enclosing the draft letter prepared in Task 7 above. Use the blank memo form on page 179 of the answer booklet.

**Monthly sales during the years ended 31 March 2002 and 31 March 2003**

All figures in £000. All figures exclude VAT.

| | Sales Division | Manufacturing Division | | |
|---|---|---|---|---|
| | *Total* | *To external customers* | *To Sales Division* | *Total* |
| **2001/2002** | | | | |
| April | 350 | 34 | 185 | 219 |
| May | 225 | 46 | 128 | 174 |
| June | 190 | 32 | 96 | 128 |
| July | 255 | 54 | 138 | 192 |
| August | 310 | 36 | 166 | 202 |
| September | 238 | 24 | 148 | 172 |
| October | 220 | 20 | 125 | 145 |
| November | 295 | 34 | 172 | 206 |
| December | 240 | 39 | 182 | 221 |
| January | 257 | 20 | 150 | 170 |
| February | 230 | 14 | 155 | 169 |
| March | 340 | 45 | 218 | 263 |
| **2002/2003** | | | | |
| April | 339 | 42 | 197 | 239 |
| May | 189 | 53 | 119 | 172 |
| June | 223 | 14 | 109 | 123 |
| July | 295 | 44 | 214 | 258 |
| August | 280 | 50 | 176 | 226 |
| September | 265 | 34 | 138 | 172 |
| October | 219 | 12 | 119 | 131 |
| November | 322 | 50 | 170 | 220 |
| December | 316 | 39 | 180 | 219 |
| January | 281 | 29 | 148 | 177 |
| February | 248 | 24 | 168 | 192 |
| March | 240 | 51 | 185 | 236 |

**Industrial index: base = 100 (January 1998)**

| | | |
|---|---|---|
| 2002 | April | 123.8 |
| | May | 124.4 |
| | June | 124.9 |
| | July | 125.7 |
| | August | 126.3 |
| | September | 127.0 |
| | October | 127.5 |
| | November | 128.1 |
| | December | 128.9 |
| 2003 | January | 129.6 |
| | February | 130.2 |
| | March | 131.0 |

**Statistical information relating to year ended 31 March 2003**

| | |
|---|---|
| Production cost of Barts produced and sold in the year | £2,190,000 |
| Gross profit for the year | £1,470,000 |
| Administration costs for the year | £580,000 |
| Distribution costs for the year | £430,000 |
| Total of all other costs for the year | £150,000 |
| Net profit for the year before taxation | £310,000 |
| Net profit for the previous year before taxation | £278,000 |
| Total capital employed | £6,590,000 |
| Number of Barts produced and sold in the year | 199,000 |
| Average number of employees in the year | 143 |

The following details have been extracted from the company's daybooks. (All figures are exclusive of VAT.)

**SALES DAY BOOK TOTALS**
**QUARTER ENDED 31 MARCH 2003**

| | January | February | March | Total |
|---|---|---|---|---|
| | £ | £ | £ | £ |
| UK sales: standard rated | 282,862.57 | 245,871.89 | 269,088.11 | 797,822.57 |
| EU sales: zero-rated | 27,143.05 | 26,126.66 | 21,920.34 | 75,190.05 |
| Total | 310,005.62 | 271,998.55 | 291,008.45 | 873,012.62 |
| VAT on UK sales | 49,500.95 | 43,027.58 | 47,090.42 | 139,618.95 |

**PURCHASES DAY BOOK TOTALS**
**QUARTER ENDED 31 MARCH 2003**

| | January | February | March | Total |
|---|---|---|---|---|
| | £ | £ | £ | £ |
| Purchases/expenses | 186,007.66 | 163,265.69 | 171,295.45 | 520,568.80 |
| VAT on purchases/expenses | 32,551.34 | 28,571.50 | 29,976.70 | 91,099.54 |

A debt of £658, inclusive of VAT, was written off as bad in March 2003. The related sale was made in June 2002. Bad debt relief is now to be claimed.

## MEMO

**To:** Amir Pindhi
**From:** Sonia Liesl
**Subject:** VAT on imports
**Date:** 11 April 2003

---

As you may know, we have been in discussions with a supplier based in the Far East. We are considering importing certain components in future for use in our manufacturing activities.

Please could you remind me very briefly of the VAT implications if we decide to proceed with this. Please also draft a letter to the VAT office, in my name, requesting relevant publications so that we can be sure we account for the VAT correctly.

Thanks for your help.

# ANSWER BOOKLET

## Task 1

**Sales to external customers**
**Manufacturing and Sales divisions combined**

| | Monthly totals £'000 | Cumulative total for the year £'000 |
|---|---|---|
| **2001/2002** | | |
| April | | |
| May | | |
| June | | |
| July | | |
| August | | |
| September | | |
| October | | |
| November | | |
| December | | |
| January | | |
| February | | |
| March | | |
| **2002/2003** | | |
| April | | |
| May | | |
| June | | |
| July | | |
| August | | |
| September | | |
| October | | |
| November | | |
| December | | |
| January | | |
| February | | |
| March | | |

**Notes**

1. In the first column, enter the monthly total of external sales achieved by the two divisions.
2. In the second column, enter the cumulative total of external sales in the accounting year.

## Task 2

## Task 3

**Indexed sales to external customers**
**Manufacturing and Sales divisions combined**

| | Unadjusted totals £'000 | Index factor | Indexed totals £'000 |
|---|---|---|---|
| **2002/2003** | | | |
| April | | | |
| May | | | |
| June | | | |
| July | | | |
| August | | | |
| September | | | |
| October | | | |
| November | | | |
| December | | | |
| January | | | |
| February | | | |
| March | | | |

**Notes**

1. In the first column, insert the monthly totals of external sales calculated in Task 1.
2. In the second column, insert the index factor required to convert to March 2003 values.
3. In the third column, calculate the monthly sales in March 2003 terms (to the nearest £1,000).

**Task 4**

## LOAN APPLICATION (extract)

Name of applicant company ____________________

Latest year for which accounting information is available ____________________

*Total sales revenue*

In latest year for which accounts are available £ ____________________

In previous year £ ____________________

Percentage change (+/-) ____________________

*Net profit after all expenses, before taxation*

In latest year for which accounts are available £ ____________________

In previous year £ ____________________

Percentage change (+/-) ____________________

*Gross profit margin (%)* ____________________

*Net profit margin (%)* ____________________

*Return on capital employed (%)* ____________________

**Notes**

1. In the case of a company with a divisional structure, all figures should refer to the results of the company as a whole, not to individual divisions within the company.
2. Unless otherwise stated, all questions relate to the latest year for which accounting information is available.
3. Figures should be actual historical values, with no indexing for inflation.
4. Return on capital employed is defined as net profit for the year before taxation, divided by total capital employed.

**Task 4 (cont.)**

## MEMO

**To:**

**From:**

**Subject:**

**Date:**

**Task 5**

## MEMO

**To:**

**From:**

**Subject:**

**Date:**

## Task 6

**Value Added Tax Return**

For the period
01-01-03 to 31-03-03

For Official Use

Registration number: 625 7816 29

Period: 03 03

You could be liable to a financial penalty if your completed return and all the VAT payable are not received by the due date.

Due date: 30.04.03

For Official Use

HOMER LIMITED
SESTOS DRIVE
PANTILE TRADING ESTATE
CV32 1AW

Fold Here

Before you fill in this form please read the notes on the back and the VAT Leaflet *"Filling in your VAT return"*. Fill in all boxes clearly in ink, and write 'none' where necessary. Don't put a dash or leave any box blank. If there are no pence write "00" in the pence column. Do not enter more than one amount in any box.

For official use

| | Box | £ | p |
|---|---|---|---|
| VAT due in this period on sales and other outputs | 1 | | |
| VAT due in this period on acquisitions from other EC Member States | 2 | | |
| Total VAT due (the sum of boxes 1 and 2) | 3 | | |
| VAT reclaimed in this period on purchases and other inputs (including acquisitions from the EC) | 4 | | |
| **Net VAT to be paid to Customs or reclaimed by you (Difference between boxes 3 and 4)** | 5 | | |
| Total value of sales and all other outputs excluding any VAT. Include your box 8 figure | 6 | | 00 |
| Total value of purchases and all other inputs excluding any VAT. Include your box 9 figure | 7 | | 00 |
| Total value of all supplies of goods and related services, excluding any VAT, to other EC Member States | 8 | | 00 |
| Total value of all acquisitions of goods and related services, excluding any VAT, from other EC Member States | 9 | | 00 |

If you are enclosing a payment please tick this box. ☐

DECLARATION: You, or someone on your behalf, must sign below.

I, .................................................................... declare that the
(Full name of signatory in BLOCK LETTERS)
information given above is true and complete.

Signature.................................................... Date ..........................

**A false declaration can result in prosecution.**

**Task 7**

# HOMER LIMITED

Sestos Drive, Pantile Trading Estate CV32 1AW
Telephone: 02467 881235

Registered office: Sestos Drive, Pantile Trading Estate CV32 1AW
Registered in England, number 2007814

**Task 8**

## MEMO

**To:**

**From:**

**Subject:**

**Date:**

# AAT

## PRACTICE SIMULATION
## UNIT 7

## HODDLE LTD

This simulation was published by the AAT prior to the issue of the 2003 revised Standards. It remains completely relevant to the revised Standards for Unit 7 and is therefore a good source of practice.

SAMPLE SIMULATION

# INSTRUCTIONS

This simulation is designed to test your ability to prepare reports and returns.

The simulation contains a large volume of data which you will require in order to complete the tasks. The information you require is provided as far as possible in the sequence in which you will need to deal with it. However, you are advised to look quickly through all of the material before you begin. This will help you to familiarise yourself with the situation and the information available.

Your answers should be set out in the Answer Booklet on Pages 193 to 202 using the answer sheets provided, and if necessary the workings sheet on page 202.

You are allowed three hours to complete your work, although up to 30 minutes extra time may be allowed.

A high level of accuracy is required. Check your work before handing it in.

Correcting fluid may be used but it should be used in moderation. Errors should be crossed out neatly and clearly. You should write in black ink, not pencil.

# THE SITUATION

Your name is Sol Bellcamp and you work as an accounts assistant for a printing company, Hoddle Limited. Hoddle Limited is owned 100 per cent by another printing company, Kelly Limited. You report to the Group Accountant, Sherry Teddingham.

Hoddle Limited manufactures a wide range of printed materials such as cards, brochures and booklets. Most customers are based in the UK, but sales are also made to other countries in the European Union (EU). There are no exports to countries outside the EU. All of the company's purchases come from businesses within the UK.

Hoddle Limited is registered for VAT and it makes both standard-rated and zero-rated supplies to its UK customers. All sales to other EU countries qualify as zero-rated. The company's local VAT office is at Brendon House, 14 Abbey Street, Pexley PY2 3WR.

Kelly Limited is separately registered for VAT; there is no group registration in force. Both companies have an accounting year ending on 31 March. There are no other companies in the Kelly group.

Hoddle Limited is a relatively small company and sometimes suffers from shortage of capacity to complete customers' jobs. In these cases, the printing work is done by Kelly Limited. Kelly then sells the completed product to Hoddle for onward sale to the customer. The sale from Kelly to Hoddle is recorded in the books of each company at cost; Kelly does not charge a profit margin.

In this simulation you are concerned with the accounting year ended 31 March 2004.

- To begin with you will be required to prepare the VAT return for Hoddle Limited in respect of the quarter ended 31 March 2004.

- You will then be required to prepare certain reports, both for internal use and for an external interfirm comparison scheme, covering the whole accounting year ended 31 March 2004. These reports will treat the two companies as a single group; they will contain consolidated figures, not figures for either of the two companies separately.

Today's date is 9 April 2004.

## TASKS

1 Refer to the documents on Pages 185 and 186, which have been received from Hoddle Ltd's suppliers during March 2004. No entries have yet been made in Hoddle Ltd's books of account in respect of these documents. You are required to explain how you will treat each one of these documents when preparing Hoddle Ltd's VAT return for the period January to March 2004. Use Page 194 for your answer.

2 Refer to the sales day book summary, purchases day book summary, cash book summary and petty cash book summary on Pages 187 and 188. These have been printed out from Hoddle Ltd's computerised accounting system for the period January to March 2004. (You are reminded that these summaries do not include the documents dealt with in Task 1.) Refer also to the memo on Page 188. Using this information you are required to complete the VAT return of Hoddle Ltd for the quarter ended 31 March 2004. A blank VAT return is provided on Page 195.

3 The Group Accountant is considering adoption of the cash accounting scheme for VAT. He believes that Hoddle Limited (though not Kelly Limited) might qualify for the scheme. He has asked you to draft a letter to the VAT office, in his name, requesting certain details of the scheme. He is interested in the turnover limit for the scheme, particularly since Hoddle is a member of a group of companies, and in the effect of the scheme in dealing with bad debts. You are required to draft this letter using the blank letterhead on Page 196.

4 Refer to the profit and loss account of Kelly Limited on Page 189, which covers the period 1 January to 31 March 2004. You are required to prepare a profit and loss account for the same period in which the results of Hoddle and Kelly are consolidated. Enter your answer on the form provided on Page 197 as follows:

- Enter the results of Kelly in the first column of the form.
- Using the information already provided for earlier tasks construct the results of Hoddle Ltd and enter them in the second column. Note that Hoddle Ltd's stock at 1 January 2004 was valued at £14,638, while stock at 31 March 2004 was valued at £16,052.
- Make appropriate adjustments in the third column to eliminate the effects of trading between Kelly and Hoddle.
- Calculate the consolidated figures and enter them in the fourth column.

5 Refer to the information on Pages 189 to 192. Using this, and information already provided for earlier tasks, you are required to prepare a report for the accountant on the group results for the year ended 31 March 2004. Your report should contain the following:

- Key ratios: gross profit margin; net profit margin; return on shareholders' capital employed.
- Sales revenue for each quarter, both in actual terms and indexed to a common base.
- A pie chart showing the proportion of annual (unindexed) sales earned in each quarter.

Use Page 198 to set out your answer. **Note that you are not required to comment on the results for the year, merely to present them according to the instructions above.**

6 You are required to complete the interfirm comparison form on Page 199.

7 You are required to prepare a memo to the group accountant enclosing the interfirm comparison form for authorisation before despatch. Use Page 201.

# Engineering Supplies Limited

Haddlefield Road, Blaysley CG6 6AW
Tel/fax: 01376 44531

*Hoddle Limited*
*22 Formguard Street*
*Pexley*
*PY6 3QW*

**SALES INVOICE NO:** *2155*

**Date:** *27 March 2004*

| | |
|---|---|
| VAT omitted in error from invoice no 2139 | £ |
| £2,667.30 @ 17.5% | 466.77 |
| Total due | 466.77 |

***Terms: net 30 days***

VAT registration: 318 1827 58

# *Alpha Stationery*

Ainsdale Centre, Mexton EV1 4DF
Telephone 01392 43215

26 March 2004

**1 box transparent folders: red**

| | |
|---|---|
| Total including VAT @ 17.5% | 14.84 |
| Amount tendered | 20.00 |
| Change | 5.16 |

VAT registration 356 7612 33

# JAMIESON & CO

Jamieson House, Baines Road, Gresham GM7 2PQ
Telephone: 01677 35567 Fax: 01677 57640

**PROFORMA SALES INVOICE**

VAT registration: *412 7553 67*

***Hoddle Limited***
***22 Formguard Street***
***Pexley***
***PY6 3QW***

For professional services in connection with debt collection

| | £ |
|---|---|
| Our fees | 350.00 |
| VAT | 61.25 |
| Total due | 411.25 |

*A VAT invoice will be submitted when the total due is paid in full*

**HODDLE LIMITED**
**SALES DAY BOOK SUMMARY**
**JANUARY TO MARCH 2004**

| | *January* | *February* | *March* | *Total* |
|---|---|---|---|---|
| | £ | £ | £ | £ |
| UK: Zero-rated | 20,091.12 | 22,397.00 | 23,018.55 | 65,506.67 |
| UK: Standard-rated | 15,682.30 | 12,914.03 | 15,632.98 | 44,229.31 |
| Other EU | 874.12 | 4,992.66 | 5,003.82 | 10,870.60 |
| VAT | 2,744.40 | 2,259.95 | 2,735.77 | 7,740.12 |
| Total | 39,391.94 | 42,563.64 | 46,391.12 | 128,346.70 |

**HODDLE LIMITED**
**PURCHASES DAY BOOK SUMMARY**
**JANUARY TO MARCH 2004**

| | *January* | *February* | *March* | *Total* |
|---|---|---|---|---|
| | £ | £ | £ | £ |
| Purchases | 14,532.11 | 20,914.33 | 15,461.77 | *50,908.21 |
| Distribution expenses | 4,229.04 | 3,761.20 | 5,221.43 | 13,211.67 |
| Administration expenses | 5,123.08 | 2,871.45 | 3,681.62 | 11,676.15 |
| Other expenses | 1,231.00 | 1,154.99 | 997.65 | 3,383.64 |
| VAT | 4,027.97 | 4,543.22 | 4,119.34 | 12,690.53 |
| Total | 29,143.20 | 33,245.19 | 29,481.81 | 91,870.20 |

*This figure includes £18,271 of purchases from Kelly Ltd.

**HODDLE LIMITED**
**CASH BOOK SUMMARY**
**JANUARY TO MARCH 2004**

| | *January* | *February* | *March* | *Total* |
|---|---|---|---|---|
| | £ | £ | £ | £ |
| Payments | | | | |
| To creditors | 12,901.37 | 15,312.70 | 18,712.44 | 46,926.51 |
| To petty cash | 601.40 | 555.08 | 623.81 | 1,780.29 |
| Wages/salaries | 5,882.18 | 6,017.98 | 6,114.31 | 18,014.47 |
| Total | 19,384.95 | 21,885.76 | 25,450.56 | 66,721.27 |
| | | | | |
| Receipts | | | | |
| VAT from Customs & Excise | 2,998.01 | | | 2,998.01 |
| From customers | 29,312.44 | 34,216.08 | 36,108.77 | 99,637.29 |
| Total | 32,310.45 | 34,216.08 | 36,108.77 | 102,635.30 |
| | | | | |
| Surplus for month | 12,925.50 | 12,330.32 | 10,658.21 | |
| Balance b/f | –8,712.41 | 4,213.09 | 16,543.41 | |
| Balance c/f | 4,213.09 | 16,543.41 | 27,201.62 | |

**HODDLE LIMITED**
**PETTY CASH BOOK SUMMARY**
**JANUARY TO MARCH 2004**

| | *January* | *February* | *March* | *Total* |
|---|---|---|---|---|
| | £ | £ | £ | £ |
| Payments | | | | |
| Stationery | 213.85 | 80.12 | 237.58 | 531.55 |
| Travel | 87.34 | 76.50 | 102.70 | 266.54 |
| Office expenses | 213.66 | 324.08 | 199.51 | 737.25 |
| VAT | 86.55 | 74.38 | 84.02 | 244.95 |
| Total | 601.40 | 555.08 | 623.81 | 1,780.29 |
| Receipts from cash book | 601.40 | 555.08 | 623.81 | 1,780.29 |
| Surplus for month | 0.00 | 0.00 | 0.00 | |
| Balance b/f | 200.00 | 200.00 | 200.00 | |
| Balance c/f | 200.00 | 200.00 | 200.00 | |

## MEMO

To: Sol Bellcamp
From: Sherry Teddingham
Date: 6 April 2004
Subject: Bad debt - Batty Limited

As you probably know, we have had great difficulty in persuading the above customer to pay what he owes us. We invoiced him in July 2003 for £420 plus VAT at the standard rate, but he has always disputed the debt and it looks as though we will never recover it. We wrote it off to the bad debt account in March of this year, so you should take this into account when preparing the VAT return for the quarter just ended.

**KELLY LIMITED**
**PROFIT AND LOSS ACCOUNT**
**FOR THE THREE MONTHS ENDED 31 MARCH 2004**

| | £ | £ |
|---|---|---|
| Sales to external customers | | 275,601 |
| Sales to Hoddle Limited at cost | | *20,167 |
| Total sales | | 295,768 |
| Opening stock | 28,341 | |
| Purchases | 136,095 | |
| | 164,436 | |
| Closing stock | 31,207 | |
| Cost of sales | | 133,229 |
| Gross profit | | 162,539 |
| Wages and salaries | 47,918 | |
| Distribution expenses | 28,341 | |
| Administration expenses | 30,189 | |
| Stationery | 2,541 | |
| Travel | 2,001 | |
| Office expenses | 3,908 | |
| Interest payable | 12,017 | |
| Other expenses | 11,765 | |
| | | 138,680 |
| Net profit for the period | | 23,859 |

*This figure includes £1,896 in respect of a job completed on 31 March 2001 but not delivered to Hoddle Limited until 1 April 2004. It is not included in Hoddle Ltd's purchases for the period ended 31 March.

**KELLY AND HODDLE**
**CONSOLIDATED BALANCE SHEET AT 31 MARCH 2004**

| | £ | £ |
|---|---|---|
| Fixed assets at net book value | | 1,229,348 |
| Current assets | | |
| Stock | 49,155 | |
| Trade debtors | 223,009 | |
| VAT recoverable | 13,451 | |
| Cash at bank and in hand | 40,088 | |
| | 325,703 | |
| Current liabilities | | |
| Trade creditors | 136,531 | |
| Other creditors | 11,740 | |
| | 148,271 | |
| Net current assets | | 177,432 |
| Total assets less current liabilities | | 1,406,780 |
| Long term liability | | |
| Loan repayable in 2005 | | 372,072 |
| | | 1,034,708 |
| Capital and reserves | | |
| Called up share capital | | 234,167 |
| Retained profits | | 800,541 |
| | | 1,034,708 |

**KELLY AND HODDLE**
**QUARTERLY CONSOLIDATED PROFIT AND LOSS ACCOUNTS**
**FOR THE YEAR ENDED 31 MARCH 2004**

| | *1 April 2003-<br>30 June 2003* | *1 July 2003-<br>30 September 2003* | *1 October 2003-<br>31 December 2003* | *1 January 2004-<br>31 March 2004* | *1 April 2003-<br>31 March 2004* |
|---|---|---|---|---|---|
| | £ | £ | £ | £ | £ |
| Sales | 325,719 | 275,230 | 306,321 | | |
| Cost of sales | 134,861 | 109,421 | 121,358 | | |
| Gross profit | 190,858 | 165,809 | 184,963 | | |
| Wages and salaries | 63,314 | 61,167 | 64,412 | | |
| Distribution expenses | 34,217 | 30,135 | 31,221 | | |
| Administration expenses | 34,765 | 33,012 | 36,415 | | |
| Stationery | 2,981 | 2,671 | 3,008 | | |
| Travel | 1,975 | 1,876 | 2,413 | | |
| Office expenses | 4,412 | 4,713 | 3,083 | | |
| Interest payable | 12,913 | 12,714 | 12,432 | | |
| Other expenses | 10,981 | 16,421 | 15,431 | | |
| | 165,558 | 162,709 | 168,415 | | |
| Net profit for the period | 25,300 | 3,100 | 16,548 | | |

*Note for candidates: you are advised to complete the above schedule by filling in the figures for the final quarter in the fourth column and totalling the figures to the year in the final column.*

# MEMO

To: Sol Bellcamp
From: Sherry Teddingham
Subject: Adjusting for the effects of price rises
Date: 2 April 2004

When presenting your quarterly reports on group results please include an item of information additional to that which you normally present. As well as noting sales revenue by quarter, please present quarterly sales revenue adjusted to take account of price rises.

I have identified a suitable index as follows.

| | |
|---|---|
| First quarter 2002/03 (base period) | 231.8 |
| First quarter 2003/04 | 239.3 |
| Second quarter 2003/04 | 241.5 |
| Third quarter 2003/04 | 244.0 |
| Fourth quarter 2003/04 | 241.8 |

I will keep you informed of future movements in this index.

# ANSWER BOOKLET

## Task 1

## Task 2

# Value Added Tax Return

For the period
to

For Official Use

Registration number: 578 4060 19

Period

You could be liable to a financial penalty if your completed return and all the VAT payable are not received by the due date.

Due date:

For Official Use

If you have a general enquiry or need advice please call our National Advice Service on 0845 010 9000

**ATTENTION**

If this return and any tax due are not received by the due date you may be liable to a surcharge.

If you make supplies of goods to another EC Member State you are required to complete an EC Sales List (VAT 101).

Before you fill in this form please read the notes on the back and the VAT Leaflet *"Filling in your VAT return"*. Fill in all boxes clearly in ink, and write 'none' where necessary. Don't put a dash or leave any box blank. If there are no pence write "00" in the pence column. Do not enter more than one amount in any box.

For official use

| | Box | £ | p |
|---|---|---|---|
| VAT due in this period on sales and other outputs | 1 | | |
| VAT due in this period on acquisitions from other EC Member States | 2 | | |
| Total VAT due (the sum of boxes 1 and 2) | 3 | | |
| VAT reclaimed in this period on purchases and other inputs (including acquisitions from the EC) | 4 | | |
| **Net VAT to be paid to Customs or reclaimed by you (Difference between boxes 3 and 4)** | 5 | | |
| Total value of sales and all other outputs excluding any VAT. Include your box 8 figure | 6 | | 00 |
| Total value of purchases and all other inputs excluding any VAT. Include your box 9 figure | 7 | | 00 |
| Total value of all supplies of goods and related services, excluding any VAT, to other EC Member States | 8 | | 00 |
| Total value of all acquisitions of goods and related services, excluding any VAT, from other EC Member States | 9 | | 00 |

If you are enclosing a payment please tick this box.

DECLARATION: You, or someone on your behalf, must sign below.

I, .................................................................................................... declare that the
(Full name of signatory in BLOCK LETTERS)
information given above is true and complete.

Signature.................................................................................... Date ..........................................

**A false declaration can result in prosecution.**

## Task 3

# HODDLE LIMITED

22 Formguard Street, Pexley PY6 3QW
Telephone 01682 431 4322569

Registered office: 22 Formguard Street, Pexley PY6 3QW
Registered in England, number 2314561

**Task 4**

**CONSOLIDATED PROFIT AND LOSS ACCOUNT**
**FOR THE THREE MONTHS ENDED 31 MARCH 2004**

| | Kelly £ | Hoddle £ | Adjustments £ | Consolidated £ |
|---|---|---|---|---|
| Sales | ....... | ....... | ....... | ....... |
| Opening stock | ....... | ....... | ....... | ....... |
| Purchases | ....... | ....... | ....... | ....... |
| | ....... | ....... | ....... | ....... |
| Closing stock | ....... | ....... | ....... | ....... |
| Cost of sales | ....... | ....... | ....... | ....... |
| Gross profit | ....... | ....... | ....... | ....... |
| Wages and salaries | ....... | ....... | ....... | ....... |
| Distribution expenses | ....... | ....... | ....... | ....... |
| Administration expenses | ....... | ....... | ....... | ....... |
| Stationery | ....... | ....... | ....... | ....... |
| Travel | ....... | ....... | ....... | ....... |
| Office expenses | ....... | ....... | ....... | ....... |
| Interest payable | ....... | ....... | ....... | ....... |
| Other expenses | ....... | ....... | ....... | ....... |
| | ....... | ....... | ....... | ....... |
| Net profit for the period | ....... | ....... | ....... | ....... |

## Task 5

## Task 6

### INTERFIRM COMPARISON DATA (extracts)

Name of company ....................................................

Year ended ..........................................................

**Data**

| | £ | *% of sales* | *Industry best* | *Industry average* |
|---|---|---|---|---|
| Sales | | | | |
| Gross profit | | | 62.1% | 57.3% |
| Net profit | | | 10.4% | 5.8% |
| Fixed assets | | | | |
| Current assets | | | | |
| Current liabilities | | | | |
| Return on capital employed | | | 10.3% | 9.0% |

**Important note**

Before completing this form you should read the explanatory notes on page 198.

## COMPLETING THE IFC DATA FORM

### Explanatory notes

Note 1

'Sales' means sales to external customers. Inter-company, inter-divisional or inter-branch sales should be excluded.

Note 2

Fixed assets should be stated at net book value.

Note 3

Return on capital employed is net profit before interest charges, divided by the total of fixed assets (stated at net book value) and net current assets.

**Task 7**

# Workings sheet

# ANSWERS

# answers to chapter 1: COSTING INFORMATION

1 Financial accounting is the recording of historical, or past, transactions of the business in order to be able to produce a set of financial statements in accordance with legal and accounting professional requirements. These financial statements are required by law for limited companies and are prepared for the use of those outside the business such as shareholders, lenders, customers and suppliers.

Cost accounting is the recording of historical, or past, transactions of the business in order to provide useful information for the management of the business in order to carry out their functions of decision making, planning and control. The costing information can be presented in any manner which is useful to management as it is used solely by the management team within the business.

2 **Decision making** – many of the decisions that management will be required to make will be to do with production and sales of their products. Decisions will have to be made as to whether to produce a product in the first place – for this it will be necessary to know what the product is going to cost to make, what selling price can be set for it and therefore whether it is going to be profitable. Costing information will show the anticipated cost of the product and can also be used to set the selling price of the product if this is not dependent on market forces. In other instances management may have to make decisions about the levels of production for which they will need costs for different amounts of production. Management may also have to choose between products if there is competition for resources such as factory space or labour hours. Again detailed information about the costs of the products is required if an informed decision is to be made.

**Planning** – once a decision has been taken to make a new product in the next period or to continue production of an existing one then a plan or budget will be drawn up. Budgets contain the details of the quantities and costs of production. They will include budgets for the quantity of materials required, the cost of those materials, the number of labour hours required, the cost of the labour and estimates of all the overheads of the business for the period.

**Control** – control of costs is a vital element of management's role. One method of control is to compare the actual costs for a period to the budgeted costs for the same period. Any differences between actual cost and budgeted costs are known as variances and any significant variances should be investigated in order to determine their cause and to alter either the budgets or future operations in the light of the variances.

**3** i) The expenditure of a business can be classified as either capital expenditure or revenue expenditure. Capital expenditure is expenditure on the purchase of assets for long term use within the business, fixed assets. Revenue expenditure is all other expenditure of the business, the day to day purchases and running costs of the business.

ii) Costs of a business can also be classified according to the function of the business that caused the cost. The main functions in manufacturing businesses are usually production, selling and distribution and administration. Costs will therefore be classified as production costs, selling and distribution costs or administration costs.

iii) Costs can be classified according to their relationship with the product that a business makes or the unit of service that it provides. If the cost can be directly identified with a unit of production or service then it is known as a direct cost. All other costs which cannot be directly identified with the unit of production or service are known as indirect costs. When classifying costs in this manner it is usual to split the direct and indirect costs into three categories, materials, labour and expenses.

iv) Some costs of a business will tend to alter as activity levels change whilst others will remain constant despite a change in activity levels. This is what is meant by analysing costs according to behaviour. If a cost remains constant irrespective of the level of activity then it is known as a fixed cost. If the cost varies directly with the level of activity then it is classified as a variable cost. Some costs have both a fixed and a variable element - this means that there is a fixed element that must be paid no matter what the level of activity and then there is a further element of the cost which will alter as activity levels alter. These costs are known as semi-variable costs. A further classification of cost is a step fixed cost. This is a cost that is fixed for a range of activity levels but outside this range will alter and then remain fixed for a further range of activity levels.

**4**

| | *Capital* | *Revenue* |
|---|---|---|
| Purchase of a car for resale by a car dealer | | ✓ |
| Purchase of a car for use by a salesman | ✓ | |
| Road tax payable on purchase of a car for use by a salesman | | ✓ |
| Redecorating of head office | | ✓ |
| Installing new machinery | ✓ | |
| Cleaning of new machinery after initial use | | ✓ |

**5**

| | Production cost | Selling and distribution cost | Administration cost |
|---|---|---|---|
| Depreciation of salesmen's cars | | ✓ | |
| Production manager's salary | ✓ | | |
| Depreciation of machinery | ✓ | | |
| Rent of office space | | | ✓ |
| Depreciation of delivery vans | | ✓ | |
| Discs for office computer | | | ✓ |

**6**

| | Direct cost | Indirect cost |
|---|---|---|
| Wages of factory supervisor | | ✓ |
| Hire of plant for construction of a building by a building firm | ✓ | |
| Cleaning materials used in the factory | | ✓ |
| Factory rent | | ✓ |
| Wages of a trainee accountant in an accountancy firm | ✓ | |
| Cement used for construction of a building by a building firm | ✓ | |

**7**

i) Semi-variable cost
ii) Fixed cost
iii) Variable cost
iv) Fixed cost
v) Step fixed cost

**8**

| | Units | Cost £ |
|---|---|---|
| Highest level – June | 145,000 | 424,000 |
| Lowest level – April | 110,000 | 340,000 |
| Increase | 35,000 | 84,000 |

Variable element of cost = $\dfrac{£84,000}{35,000 \text{ units}}$

= £2.40 per unit

| | £ |
|---|---|
| June production – variable costs (145,000 x £2.40) | 348,000 |
| Fixed costs (balancing figure) | 76,000 |
| Total production cost | 424,000 |

**9**

| | *80,000 units* £ | *130,000 units* £ | *180,000 units* £ |
|---|---|---|---|
| Variable costs – production costs (£3.80 + 1.40 + 0.30 = £5.50) | 440,000 | 715,000 | 990,000 |
| Fixed cost – depreciation | 30,000 | 30,000 | 30,000 |
| Step fixed cost – rent | 150,000 | 190,000 | 190,000 |
| | 620,000 | 935,000 | 1,210,000 |

# answers to chapter 2: MATERIALS COSTS

**1** i) The three main categories of stock for a manufacturing business are **raw materials, work in progress** and **finished goods**

ii) The internal document used to record the quantity of materials received from a supplier is known as a **goods received note**

iii) The initial internal document that starts the purchasing process for materials is known as a **purchase requisition**

iv) A **purchase order** is the document that is sent to a supplier to request the supply of materials

v) When materials are required from stores by the factory a **materials requisition** is filled out

vi) A **purchase invoice** is the document received from a supplier of materials requesting payment

**2**

## BIN CARD

**Description:** 23 Electrical component EC23 **Bin No:** 413

**Code No:**

| Receipts | | | Issues | | | Balance |
|---|---|---|---|---|---|---|
| Date | Reference | Quantity | Date | Reference | Quantity | Quantity |
| 2003<br>1 June | | | | | | 50 |
| 3 June | GRN0326 | 340 | | | | 390 |
| | | | 5 June | MR0295 | 150 | 240 |
| | | | 10 June | MR0307 | 190 | 50 |
| 12 June | GRN0348 | 300 | | | | 350 |
| | | | 20 June | MR0315 | 180 | 170 |
| | | | 25 June | MR0320 | 100 | 70 |
| 28 June | GRN0363 | 320 | | | | 390 |

**3** i) FIFO

**STORES LEDGER ACCOUNT**

Stock item XK2

Code 041861

| Date | Receipts | | | | Issues | | | | Balance | |
|---|---|---|---|---|---|---|---|---|---|---|
| | GRN | Qty | Unit price £ | £ | Req No | Qty | Unit price £ | £ | Qty | £ |
| 1 July | | | | | | | | | 400 | 1,200.00 |
| 4 July | | | | | 416 | 320 | 3.00 | 960 | 80 | 240.00 |
| 7 July | 668 | 500 | 3.20 | 1,600 | | | | | 580 | 1,840.00 |
| 12 July | | | | | 422 | 80 | 3.00 | 240 | | |
| | | | | | | 100 | 3.20 | 320 | 400 | 1,280.00 |
| 16 July | | | | | 428 | 300 | 3.20 | 960 | 100 | 320.00 |
| 19 July | 674 | 500 | 3.50 | 1,750 | | | | | 600 | 2,070.00 |
| 23 July | | | | | 433 | 100 | 3.20 | 320 | | |
| | | | | | | 130 | 3.50 | 455 | 370 | 1,295.00 |
| 28 July | | | | | 440 | 300 | 3.50 | 1,050 | 70 | 245.00 |

ii) LIFO

## STORES LEDGER ACCOUNT

Stock item XK2

Code 041861

| Date | Receipts | | | | Issues | | | | Balance | |
|---|---|---|---|---|---|---|---|---|---|---|
| | GRN | Qty | Unit price £ | £ | Req No | Qty | Unit price £ | £ | Qty | £ |
| 1 July | | | | | | | | | 400 | 1,200.00 |
| 4 July | | | | | 416 | 320 | 3.00 | 960 | 80 | 240.00 |
| 7 July | 668 | 500 | 3.20 | 1,600 | | | | | 580 | 1,840.00 |
| 12 July | | | | | 422 | 180 | 3.20 | 576 | 400 | 1,264.00 |
| 16 July | | | | | 428 | 300 | 3.20 | 960 | 100 | 304.00 |
| 19 July | 674 | 500 | 3.50 | 1,750 | | | | | 600 | 2,054.00 |
| 23 July | | | | | 433 | 230 | 3.50 | 805 | 370 | 1,249.00 |
| 28 July | | | | | 440 | 270 | 3.50 | 945 | | |
| | | | | | | 20 | 3.20 | 64 | 70 | |
| | | | | | | 10 | 3.00 | 30 | | 210.00 |

iii) Weighted average cost

**STORES LEDGER ACCOUNT**

Stock item XK2

Code 041861

| Date | Receipts | | | | Issues | | | | Balance | |
|---|---|---|---|---|---|---|---|---|---|---|
| | GRN | Qty | Unit price £ | £ | Req No | Qty | Unit price £ | £ | Qty | £ |
| 1 July | | | | | | | | | 400 | 1,200.00 |
| 4 July | | | | | 416 | 320 | 3.00 | 960 | 80 | 240.00 |
| 7 July | 668 | 500 | 3.20 | 1,600 | | | | | 580 | 1,840.00 |
| 12 July | | | | | 422 | 180 | 3.17 | 570 | 400 | 1,269.40 |
| 16 July | | | | | 428 | 300 | 3.17 | 951 | 100 | 318.40 |
| 19 July | 674 | 500 | 3.50 | 1,750 | | | | | 600 | 2,068.40 |
| 23 July | | | | | 433 | 230 | 3.45 | 793 | 370 | 1,274.90 |
| 28 July | | | | | 440 | 300 | 3.45 | 1,035 | 70 | 239.90 |

**WORKINGS**

Calculation of weighted average price:

| | | | | £ |
|---|---|---|---|---|
| 4 July | 80 | @ | 3.00 | 240.00 |
| 7 July | 500 | @ | 3.20 | 1,600.00 |
| | 580 | | 3.17 | 1,840.00 |
| 12 July | (180) | @ | 3.17 | (570.60) |
| 16 July | (300) | @ | 3.17 | (951.00) |
| 19 July | 500 | @ | 3.50 | 1,750.00 |
| | 600 | @ | 3.45 | 2,068.40 |
| 23 July | (230) | @ | 3.45 | (793.50) |
| 28 July | (300) | @ | 3.45 | (1,035.00) |
| | 70 | @ | 3.45 | 239.90 |

**4 FIFO**

| | | | | | £ |
|---|---|---|---|---|---|
| 1 July | Opening balance | 220 | @ | 5.60 | 1,232.00 |
| 3 July | Issue | (160) | @ | 5.60 | (896.00) |
| | | 60 | | | 336.00 |
| 7 July | Purchase | 300 | @ | 6.00 | 1,800.00 |
| | | 360 | | | 2,136.00 |
| 10 July | Issue | (60) | @ | 5.60 | ( 336.00) |
| | | (110) | @ | 6.00 | (660.00) |
| | | 190 | | | 1,140.00 |
| 15 July | Issue | (100) | @ | 6.00 | (600.00) |
| | | 90 | | | 540.00 |
| 20 July | Purchase | 250 | @ | 6.30 | 1,575.00 |
| | | 340 | | | 2,115.00 |
| 24 July | Issue | (90) | @ | 6.00 | (540.00) |
| | | (110) | @ | 6.30 | (693.00) |
| | | 140 | | | 882.00 |

i) Cost of issues (£896.00 + 336.00 + 660.00 + 600.00 + 540.00 + 693.00) = £3,725.00

ii) Closing stock value = £882.00

**LIFO**

| | | | | | |
|---|---|---|---|---|---|
| 1 July | Opening balance | 220 | @ | 5.60 | 1,232.00 |
| 3 July | Issue | (160) | @ | 5.60 | (896.00) |
| | | 60 | | | 336.00 |
| 7 July | Purchase | 300 | @ | 6.00 | 1,800.00 |
| | | 360 | | | 2,136.00 |
| 10 July | Issue | (170) | @ | 6.00 | (1,020.00) |
| | | 190 | | | 1,116.00 |
| 15 July | Issue | (100) | @ | 6.00 | (600.00) |
| | | 90 | | | 516.00 |
| 20 July | Purchase | 250 | @ | 6.30 | 1,575.00 |
| | | 340 | | | 2,091.00 |
| 24 July | Issue | (200) | @ | 6.30 | (1,260.00) |
| | | 140 | | | 831.00 |

i) Cost of issues (£896.00 + 1,020.00 + 600.00 + 1,260.00) = £3,776.00

ii) Closing stock value = £831.00

**Weighted average cost**

| | | | | | |
|---|---|---|---|---|---|
| 1 July | Opening balance | 220 | @ | 5.60 | 1,232.00 |
| 3 July | Issue | (160) | @ | 5.60 | (896.00) |
| | | 60 | | | 336.00 |
| 7 July | Purchase | 300 | @ | 6.00 | 1,800.00 |
| | | 360 | | 5.93 | 2,136.00 |
| 10 July | Issue | (170) | @ | 5.93 | (1,008.10) |
| 15 July | Issue | (100) | @ | 5.93 | ( 593.00) |
| 20 July | Purchase | 250 | @ | 6.30 | 1,575.00 |
| | | 340 | | 6.21 | 2,109.90 |
| 24 July | Issue | (200) | @ | 6.21 | (1,242.00) |
| | | 140 | @ | 6.21 | 867.90 |

i) Cost of issues (£896.00 + 1,008.10 + 593.00 + 1,242.00) = £3,739.10

ii) Closing stock value = £867.90

**5** The FIFO method of stock valuation makes the assumption that each time an issue is made from stock that this issue is of the earliest purchases which will often reflect the actual usage pattern as the oldest stocks will often be used first. This means that at the end of the period the closing stocks are valued at the most recent up-to-date prices. However this method also means that the cost of issues to production are made at varying different and possibly out-of -date prices – this in turn means that the profit shown, if prices are rising, will be higher than that under the LIFO method.

The LIFO method of stock valuation makes the assumption that each time an issue is made from stock that this issue is of the most recent purchases – effectively therefore the issue is being made from the top of the pile of stock which may reflect actual practice. Issues are therefore made at current up-to-date prices which means that managers are more aware of current prices as these are the ones that their department is being charged. However as with FIFO it does mean that the price being charged for issues is constantly changing. The closing stock under LIFO is valued at the earliest prices and therefore may be an extremely out of date figure. As issues are charged at current prices the profit shown under LIFO, if prices are rising, will be lower than that under FIFO and indeed this method is not recommended for use in the financial statements by SSAP 9.

**6**

Materials control account

| | £ | | £ |
|---|---|---|---|
| Opening stock | 12,523 | WIP | 79,247 |
| Creditors | 83,469 | Production overhead control | 6,248 |
| | | Closing stock | 10,497 |
| | 95,992 | | 95,992 |

Work in progress control account

| | £ | | £ |
|---|---|---|---|
| Materials control | 79,247 | | |

Production overhead control account

| | £ | | £ |
|---|---|---|---|
| Materials control | 6,248 | | |

7 a) Re-order level = maximum demand x maximum lead time

= 200 x 8

= 1,600 units

b) EOQ = $\sqrt{\frac{2cd}{h}}$

= $\sqrt{\frac{2 \times £100 \times 40{,}000}{2}}$

= 2,000 units

c) Minimum stock level = re-order level – (average usage x average lead time)

= 1,600 – (160 x 5)

= 800 units

d) Maximum stock level = re-order level + re-order quantity – (minimum usage x minimum lead time)

= 1,600 + 2,000 – (130 x 2)

= 3,340 units

# answers to chapter 3: LABOUR COSTS AND EXPENSES

**1** i)

| | £ |
|---|---|
| Basic pay 37 hours @ £6.80 | 251.60 |
| Overtime pay 6 hours @ £6.80 x 1.5 | 61.20 |
| Total gross pay | 312.80 |

ii) Overtime payment £61.20

iii) Overtime premium £6.80 x 0.5 x 6 hours £20.40

**2**

| | £ |
|---|---|
| 300 units @ £1.00 | 300.00 |
| 100 units @ £1.15 | 115.00 |
| 30 units @ £1.35 | 40.50 |
| Total gross pay | 455.50 |

**3** i) Harry

| | £ |
|---|---|
| Product A £10.40 x 22 | 228.80 |
| Product B £18.60 x 7 | 130.20 |
| Total gross pay | 359.00 |

ii) Stella

| | |
|---|---|
| Basic pay 35 hours @ £8.40 | 294.00 |
| Overtime pay 8 hours @ £8.40 x 1 1/3 | 89.60 |
| Total gross pay | 383.60 |

iii) Yvette

| | |
|---|---|
| Basic salary £20,000/12 | 1,666.67 |
| Bonus £20,000 x 5% | 1,000.00 |
| Total gross pay | 2,666.67 |

**4**

Wages control account

| | £ | | £ |
|---|---|---|---|
| Bank | 24,700 | WIP | 20,900 |
| Inland Revenue | 6,200 | Production overheads | 12,400 |
| Pension scheme | 2,400 | | |
| | 33,300 | | 33,300 |

Work in progress control account

| | £ | | £ |
|---|---|---|---|
| Wages control | 20,900 | | |

Production overhead control account

| | £ | | £ |
|---|---|---|---|
| Wages control | 12,400 | | |

**5** Freehold building $= \dfrac{£450{,}000 - 50{,}000}{40 \text{ years}}$

$= £10{,}000$

Machinery $= (£220{,}000 - 20{,}000) \times \dfrac{4{,}200}{32{,}000}$

$= £26{,}250$

Cars $= (£120{,}000 - 52{,}500) \times 25\%$

$= £16{,}875$

**6**

Work in progress control account

| | £ | | £ |
|---|---|---|---|
| Direct production costs | 7,200 | | |

Production overhead control account

| | £ | | £ |
|---|---|---|---|
| Indirect production costs | 39,256 | | |

# answers to chapter 4: OVERHEADS

**1**

| | *Total* | *Assembly* | *Finishing* | *Stores* | *Maintenance* |
|---|---|---|---|---|---|
| | £ | £ | £ | £ | £ |
| Indirect materials | 18,700 | 16,500 | 2,200 | | |
| Indirect labour | 22,800 | 7,500 | 6,200 | 4,500 | 4,600 |
| Rent and rates | 10,000 | 3,000 | 2,000 | 2,500 | 2,500 |
| Heat and light | 7,400 | 2,220 | 1,480 | 1,850 | 1,850 |
| Supervisor's wages | 9,880 | 5,720 | 4,160 | – | – |
| Depreciation of machinery | 8,400 | 5,250 | 1,750 | 525 | 875 |
| | 77,180 | 40,190 | 17,790 | 9,375 | 9,825 |
| Stores | | 6,875 | 2,500 | (9,375) | |
| Maintenance | | 5,731 | 4,094 | | (9,825) |
| | | 52,796 | 24,384 | – | – |

**WORKINGS**

Rent and rates and light and heat are apportioned on the basis of floor area – assembly 30%, finishing 20%, stores and maintenance 25% each.

Supervisor's wages are apportioned on the basis of the supervisor's time in each department – 22:16

Depreciation is apportioned on the basis of net book value – 150:50:15:25

The stores overheads are then reapportioned on the basis of the number of materials requisitions and the maintenance overheads on the basis of the number of maintenance hours required.

**2**

| | Total | A | B | Stores | Canteen |
|---|---|---|---|---|---|
| | £ | £ | £ | £ | £ |
| Indirect wages | 75,700 | 7,800 | 4,700 | 21,200 | 42,000 |
| Rent | 24,000 | 9,600 | 6,400 | 3,200 | 4,800 |
| Buildings insurance | 2,000 | 800 | 533 | 267 | 400 |
| Power | 6,400 | 2,880 | 1,920 | 320 | 1,280 |
| Heat and light | 4,000 | 1,600 | 1,066 | 534 | 800 |
| Supervisor's wages | 10,000 | 6,250 | 3,750 | – | – |
| Machinery depreciation | 3,200 | 1,493 | 1,280 | 160 | 267 |
| Machinery insurance | 2,200 | 1,027 | 880 | 110 | 183 |
| | 127,500 | 31,450 | 20,529 | 25,791 | 49,730 |
| Canteen | | 29,009 | 16,577 | 4,144 | (49,730) |
| | | | | 29,935 | |
| Stores | | 17,961 | 11,974 | (29,935) | |
| | | 78,420 | 49,080 | – | – |

**WORKINGS**

Rent, buildings insurance and heat and light are apportioned on the basis of floor area – 12:8:4:6

Power is apportioned using the percentages given

Supervisor's wages are apportioned according to the hours to be spent in each cost centre 25:15

Machinery depreciation and insurance are apportioned on the basis of the net book value of the machinery – 140:120:15:25

Canteen costs are apportioned according to the number of staff that use it – 70:40:10

The stores costs are apportioned on the basis of the number of materials requisitions.

**3**

| | Total | Assembly | Polishing | Stores | Maintenance |
|---|---|---|---|---|---|
| | £ | £ | £ | £ | £ |
| | 130,000 | 60,000 | 40,000 | 20,000 | 10,000 |
| Stores | | 10,000 | 8,000 | (20,000) | 2,000 |
| | | | | – | 12,000 |
| Maintenance | | 7,200 | 4,800 | | (12,000) |
| | 130,000 | 77,200 | 52,800 | – | – |

**4**

| | | *Cutting* | *Finishing* |
|---|---|---|---|
| i) | Rate per unit | $\frac{58,600}{10,000}$ | $\frac{42,400}{10,000}$ |
| | = | £5.86 per unit | £4.24 per unit |

- can be used where all products are of similar size and require a similar input in terms of time and resources of the departments

| | | *Cutting* | *Finishing* |
|---|---|---|---|
| ii) | Rate per direct labour hour | $\frac{58,600}{4,000}$ | $\frac{42,400}{24,000}$ |
| | = | £14.65 per labour hour | £1.77 per labour hour |

- most appropriate in labour intensive departments where most of the overhead relates to labour

| | | *Cutting* | *Finishing* |
|---|---|---|---|
| iii) | Rate per machine hour | $\frac{58,600}{12,000}$ | $\frac{42,400}{2,000}$ |
| | = | £4.88 per machine hour | £21.20 per machine hour |

- most appropriate in a largely mechanised department where most of the overhead relates to machinery costs

**5** i) C = $\frac{£125,000}{100,000}$

= £1.25 per machine hour

- as C is a highly mechanised department most of the overhead will relate to the machinery therefore machine hours have been used to absorb the overhead.

D = $\frac{£180,000}{80,000}$

= £2.25 per direct labour hour

- as D is a highly labour intensive department then most of the overhead will relate to the hours that are worked by the labour force therefore labour hours are used to absorb the overhead.

| | | | | |
|---|---|---|---|---|
| ii) | Product P - department C overhead | £1.25 x 5 | = | £ 6.25 |
| | department D overhead | £2.25 x 7 | = | £15.75 |

**6** i) Overhead absorption rate = $\frac{£5,400}{1,200}$

= £4.50 per unit

Overhead incurred = £5,000
Overhead absorbed
1,000 units x £4.50 = £4,500

Under-absorbed overhead = £500 – a further expense in the P&L

ii) Overhead absorption rate = $\frac{£5,040}{1,800}$

= £2.80 per direct labour hour

Overhead incurred = £5,100
Overhead absorbed
2,200 hours x £2.80 = £6,160

Over-absorbed overhead = £1,060 – a credit to the P&L

iii) Overhead absorption rate = $\frac{£320,000}{80,000}$

= £4.00 per machine hour

Overhead incurred = £320,000
Overhead absorbed
82,000 x £4.00 = £328,000

Over-absorbed overhead = £8,000 – a credit to the P&L

**7** i)

Production overhead control account

| | £ | | £ |
|---|---|---|---|
| Creditors/cash – overheads incurred | 5,000 | WIP – overheads absorbed | 4,500 |
| | | P&L – under absorbed | 500 |

ii)

Production overhead control account

| | £ | | £ |
|---|---|---|---|
| Creditors/cash – overheads incurred | 5,100 | WIP – overheads absorbed | 6,160 |
| P&L – over absorbed | 1,060 | | |
| | 6,160 | | 6,160 |

iii)

Production overhead control account

| | £ | | £ |
|---|---|---|---|
| Creditors/cash – overheads incurred | 320,000 | WIP – overheads absorbed | 328,000 |
| P&L – over absorbed | 8,000 | | |
| | 328,000 | | 328,000 |

# answers to chapter 5: ABSORPTION COSTING AND MARGINAL COSTING

**1 Absorption costing**

| | £ |
|---|---|
| Direct materials | 12.00 |
| Direct labour – cutting (2 x £7.40) | 14.80 |
| finishing | 6.80 |
| Variable overheads: | |
| Cutting ((£336,000/240,000) x 2) | 2.80 |
| Finishing (£132,000/120,000) | 1.10 |
| Fixed overheads: | |
| Cutting ((£144,000/240,000) x 2) | 1.20 |
| Finishing (£96,000/120,000) | 0.80 |
| | 39.50 |

**Marginal costing**

| | £ |
|---|---|
| Direct materials | 12.00 |
| Direct labour – cutting (2 x £7.40) | 14.80 |
| finishing | 6.80 |
| Variable overheads: | |
| Cutting (£336,000/240,000 x 2) | 2.80 |
| Finishing (£132,000/120,000) | 1.10 |
| | 37.50 |

**2 Cost per unit - absorption costing**

| | £ |
|---|---|
| Direct materials | 6.80 |
| Direct labour | 3.60 |
| Variable costs (£32,400/24,000) | 1.35 |
| Fixed costs (£44,400/24,000) | 1.85 |
| | 13.60 |

**Cost per unit - marginal costing**

| | £ |
|---|---|
| Direct materials | 6.80 |
| Direct labour | 3.60 |
| Variable costs (£32,400/24,000) | 1.35 |
| | 11.75 |

a) **Absorption costing - profit and loss account**

| | July £ | July £ | August £ | August £ |
|---|---|---|---|---|
| Sales (22,000 x £16) | | 352,000 | | |
| (25,000 x £16) | | | | 400,000 |
| Less: cost of sales | | | | |
| Opening stock (1,500 x £13.60) | 20,400 | | | |
| (3,500 x £13.60) | | | 47,600 | |
| Production (24,000 x £13.60) | 326,400 | | 326,400 | |
| | 346,800 | | 374,000 | |
| Less: closing stock (3,500 x £13.60) | (47,600) | | | |
| (2,500 x £13.60) | | | (34,000) | |
| | | 299,200 | | 340,000 |
| Profit | | 52,800 | | 60,000 |

**Marginal costing - profit and loss account**

| | July £ | July £ | August £ | August £ |
|---|---|---|---|---|
| Sales (22,000 x £16) | | 352,000 | | |
| (25,000 x £16) | | | | 400,000 |
| Less: cost of sales | | | | |
| Opening stock (1,500 x £11.75) | 17,625 | | | |
| (3,500 x £11.75) | | | 41,125 | |
| Production (24,000 x £11.75) | 282,000 | | 282,000 | |
| | 299,625 | | 323,125 | |
| Less: closing stock (3,500 x £11.75) | (41,125) | | | |
| (2,500 x £11.75) | | | (29,375) | |
| | | 258,500 | | 293,750 |
| Contribution | | 93,500 | | 106,250 |
| Fixed costs | | 44,400 | | 44,400 |
| | | 49,100 | | 61,850 |

b) **Reconciliation of profit figures**

| | | *July* | *August* |
|---|---|---|---|
| | | £ | £ |
| Absorption cost profit | | 52,800 | 60,000 |
| Increase in stock | (3,500 – 1,500) | | |
| x fixed c.p.u. | 2,000 x £1.85 | (3,700) | |
| Decrease in stock | (3,500 – 2,500) | | |
| x fixed c.p.u. | 1,000 x £1.85 | | 1,850 |
| | | 49,100 | 61,850 |

**3 Unit cost - absorption costing**

| | £ |
|---|---|
| Direct materials | 23.60 |
| Direct labour (4 x £5.80) | 23.20 |
| Variable overheads (£88,000/8,000) | 11.00 |
| Fixed overheads (£51,200/8,000) | 6.40 |
| | 64.20 |

**Unit cost - marginal costing**

| | £ |
|---|---|
| Direct materials | 23.60 |
| Direct labour (4 x £5.80) | 23.20 |
| Variable overheads (£88,000/8,000) | 11.00 |
| | 57.80 |

**a) Absorption costing - profit and loss account**

| | £ | £ |
|---|---|---|
| Sales (8,200 x £70) | | 574,000 |
| Less: cost of sales | | |
| Opening stock (840 x £64.20) | 53,928 | |
| Production cost (8,000 x £64.20) | 513,600 | |
| | 567,528 | |
| Less: closing stock (640 x £64.20) | 41,088 | |
| | | 526,440 |
| Profit | | 47,560 |

**Marginal costing - profit and loss account**

| | £ | £ |
|---|---|---|
| Sales (8,200 x £70) | | 574,000 |
| Less: cost of sales | | |
| Opening stock (840 x £57.80) | 48,552 | |
| Production cost (8,000 x £57.80) | 462,400 | |
| | 510,952 | |
| Less: closing stock (640 x £57.80) | 36,992 | |
| | | 473,960 |
| Contribution | | 100,040 |
| Less: fixed costs | | 51,200 |
| Profit | | 48,840 |

b)

| | £ |
|---|---|
| Absorption costing profit | 47,560 |
| Decrease in stocks x fixed cost per unit (200 x £6.40) | 1,280 |
| Marginal costing profit | 48,840 |

**4** Absorption costing has the advantage of allowing managers to see whether the sales of their products are covering all of the production costs of those products. However, due to the different nature of fixed costs compared with variable costs, it is argued that contribution is a much more useful figure for management than a profit figure after production overheads have been apportioned. If fixed costs are included in the cost per unit then the unit cost will fall as activity levels increase simply due to the nature of the fixed cost not changing but being spread over more units of activity.

A further argument for the use of marginal costing rather than absorption costing for cost reporting purposes is to do with the profit differences and stock levels. Under absorption costing we have seen that it is possible to report a higher profit figure by increasing the closing stock levels. If a manager is assessed and possibly remunerated on the basis of the figure that he reports for profit then the profit can be manipulated by over producing and building up stock levels. Although this will increase absorption costing profit it may not be in the best interests of the organisation. This type of manipulation of profit cannot take place if marginal costing is used.

# answers to chapter 6: COSTING SYSTEMS

**1** Job costing is an appropriate costing system in the type of business where the product that is produced is a 'one-off' job for a customer. Each individual job will tend to be different and have different materials, labour and expenses inputs. Therefore the costs of each individual job need to be specified.

**2** **Job costing schedule**

| | £ |
|---|---|
| Direct materials | 2,800.00 |
| Direct labour | 526.50 |
| Overheads | 234.90 |
| Total costs | 3,561.40 |
| Profit (20% x 3,561.40) | 712.28 |
| | 4,273.68 |
| VAT | 747.89 |
| Total price | 5,021.57 |

**3** **JOB NUMBER 2856**

| | *Budget* £ | *Actual* £ | *Variance* £ |
|---|---|---|---|
| Direct materials | | | |
| ■ wood | 1,650.00 | 1,830.00 | 180.00 ADV |
| ■ components | 830.00 | 755.00 | 75.00 FAV |
| ■ plastic | 320.00 | 300.00 | 20.00 FAV |
| Direct labour | | | |
| ■ Grade I - 30hours | 414.00 | 478.50 | 64.50 ADV |
| ■ Grade III - 12 hours | 132.00 | 77.00 | 55.00 FAV |
| Direct expenses | | | |
| ■ hire of equipment | 300.00 | 380.00 | 80.00 ADV |
| Overheads 42 x £4.60 | 193.20 | | |
| 40 x £4.60 | | 184.00 | 9.20 FAV |
| Total cost | 3,839.20 | 4,004.50 | 165.30 ADV |
| Profit (3,839.20 x 25%) | 959.80 | | |
| (4,799.00 – 4,004.50) | | 794.50 | |
| | 4,799.00 | 4,799.00 | |
| VAT | 839.82 | 839.82 | |
| Job Cost | 5,638.82 | 5,638.82 | |

**4** **Step 1** Calculate the number of normal loss units:
100,000 kg x 6% = 6,000 kg

**Step 2** Calculate the expected output from the process:
100,000 kg – 6,000 kg = 94,000 kg

**Step 3** Total the process costs:
£287,000 + 138,000 + 82,600 = £507,600

**Step 4** Calculate the cost per unit of expected output:

$$\frac{£507,600}{94,000} = £5.40 \text{ per kg}$$

Process account

| | kg | £ | | kg | £ |
|---|---|---|---|---|---|
| Materials | 100,000 | 287,000 | Normal loss | 6,000 | - |
| Labour | | 138,000 | Abnormal loss | 2,000 | 10,800 |
| Overheads | | 82,600 | Output | 92,000 | 496,800 |
| | 100,000 | 507,600 | | 100,000 | 507,600 |

Abnormal loss account

| | kg | £ | | kg | £ |
|---|---|---|---|---|---|
| Process account | 2,000 | 10,800 | Profit and loss | 2,000 | 10,800 |

5 **Step 1** Calculate the number of normal loss units:
18,000 ltr x 5% = 900 ltr

**Step 2** Calculate the expected output from the process:
18,000 ltr – 900 ltr = 17,100 ltr

**Step 3** Total the process costs:
£35,800 + 7,200 + 11,720 = £54,720

**Step 4** Calculate the cost per unit of expected output:

$$\frac{£54,720}{17,100} = £3.20 \text{ per litre}$$

Process account

| | ltr | £ | | ltr | £ |
|---|---|---|---|---|---|
| Materials | 18,000 | 35,800 | Normal loss | 900 | - |
| Labour | | 7,200 | Output | 17,500 | 56,000 |
| Overheads | | 11,720 | | | |
| Abnormal gain | 400 | 1,280 | | | |
| | 18,400 | 56,000 | | 18,400 | 56,000 |

Abnormal gain account

| | ltr | £ | | ltr | £ |
|---|---|---|---|---|---|
| Profit and loss | 400 | 1,280 | Process account | 400 | 1,280 |

6 **Step 1** Calculate the number of normal loss units:
50,000 kg x 10% = 5,000 kg

**Step 2** Calculate the expected output from the process:
50,000 kg – 5,000 kg = 45,000 kg

**Step 3** Total the process costs and deduct the scrap value of the normal loss:
£356,400 + 120,500 + 41,600 – (5,000 x £2) = £508,500

**Step 4** Calculate the cost per unit of expected output:

$$\frac{£508,500}{45,000} = £11.30$$

Process account

| | kg | £ | | kg | £ |
|---|---|---|---|---|---|
| Materials | 50,000 | 356,400 | Normal loss | 5,000 | 10,000 |
| Labour | | 120,500 | Output | 3,000 | 33,900 |
| Overheads | | 41,600 | | 42,000 | 474,600 |
| | | 518,500 | | | 518,000 |

Abnormal loss account

| | kg | £ | | kg | £ |
|---|---|---|---|---|---|
| Process account | 3,000 | 33,900 | Scrap proceeds | 3,000 | 6,000 |
| | | | Profit and loss | | 27,900 |
| | 3,000 | 33,900 | | 3,000 | 33,900 |

# answers to chapter 7: COST BOOKKEEPING

**1**

Production overhead control account

| | £ | | £ |
|---|---|---|---|
| Overheads incurred | 4,720 | Overheads absorbed | |
| | | 1,400 x £3.20 | 4,480 |
| | | Under absorbed overhead | 240 |
| | 4,720 | | 4,720 |

The under absorbed overhead of £240 is debited to the profit and loss account as an additional cost.

**2**

Production overhead control account

| | £ | | £ |
|---|---|---|---|
| Overheads incurred | 5,840 | Overheads absorbed | |
| Over absorbed overhead | 223 | 940 x £6.45 | 6,063 |
| | 6,063 | | 6,063 |

The over absorbed overhead of £223 will be credited to the profit and loss account.

**3**

Materials control account

| | £ | | £ |
|---|---|---|---|
| Creditors | 14,365 | WIP control | 11,632 |
| | | Closing stock | 2,733 |
| | 14,365 | | 14,365 |

Wages control account

| | £ | | £ |
|---|---|---|---|
| Gross wages (18,375 + 2,682) | 21,057 | WIP control | 18,375 |
| | | Production overhead control | 2,682 |
| | 21,057 | | 21,057 |

Production overhead control account

| | £ | | £ |
|---|---|---|---|
| Wages control | 2,682 | Overhead absorbed – WIP | |
| Bank | 6,243 | 1,530 x £5.20 | 7,956 |
| | | Under absorbed overhead | 969 |
| | 8,925 | | 8,925 |

Work in progress control account

| | £ | | £ |
|---|---|---|---|
| Materials control | 11,632 | Finished goods | 36,540 |
| Wages control | 18,375 | | |
| Production overhead | 7,956 | Closing stock | 1,423 |
| | 37,963 | | 37,963 |

**4**

i)

Materials control account

| | £ | | £ |
|---|---|---|---|
| Opening stock | 1,290 | WIP control | 6,620 |
| Creditors | 7,640 | Administration overhead | 990 |
| | | Closing stock | 1,320 |
| | 8,930 | | 8,930 |

Wages control account

| | £ | | £ |
|---|---|---|---|
| Gross wages (5,430 + 1,460) | 6,890 | WIP control | 5,430 |
| | | Production overhead control | 1,460 |
| | 6,890 | | 6,890 |

Production overhead control account

| | £ | | £ |
|---|---|---|---|
| Wages control | 1,460 | Overhead absorbed – WIP | |
| Cash | 4,290 | 490 x £11.10 | 5,439 |
| | | Under absorbed overhead (P&L) | 311 |
| | 5,750 | | 5,750 |

Work in progress control account

| | £ | | £ |
|---|---|---|---|
| Opening balance | 1,540 | Finished goods | 12,200 |
| Materials control | 6,620 | | |
| Production overhead | 5,439 | Closing balance | 1,399 |
| | 13,599 | | 13,599 |

Finished goods control account

| | £ | | £ |
|---|---|---|---|
| Opening stock | 1,830 | P&L (bal fig) | 12,380 |
| WIP control | 12,200 | Closing stock | 1,650 |
| | 14,030 | | 14,030 |

Debtors control account

| | £ | | £ |
|---|---|---|---|
| Opening balance | 7,200 | Cash | 6,800 |
| Sales | 14,700 | Closing balance | 15,100 |
| | 21,900 | | 21,900 |

Creditors control account

| | £ | | £ |
|---|---|---|---|
| Cash | 4,900 | Opening balance | 5,460 |
| Closing balance | 8,200 | Materials | 7,640 |
| | 13,100 | | 13,100 |

Cash at bank account

| | £ | | £ |
|---|---|---|---|
| Opening balance | 3,070 | Creditors | 4,900 |
| Debtors | 6,800 | Production overheads | 4,290 |
| Closing balance | 530 | Administration overheads | 1,210 |
| | 10,400 | | 10,400 |

Administration overheads account

| | £ | | £ |
|---|---|---|---|
| Materials control | 990 | | |
| Cash | 1,210 | P&L | 2,200 |
| | 2,200 | | 2,200 |

Sales account

| | £ | | £ |
|---|---|---|---|
| P&L | 14,700 | Debtors | 14,700 |

ii) **Profit and loss account**

| | £ |
|---|---|
| Sales | 14,700 |
| Cost of goods sold (finished goods) | (12,380) |
| Gross profit | 2,320 |
| Under absorbed overhead | (311) |
| Administration overheads | (2,200) |
| Net loss | (191) |

# answers to chapter 8: SHORT TERM DECISION MAKING

1 Provided that the selling price and the variable costs remain constant then contribution per unit will also be constant no matter what the level of activity. However full production cost per unit will decrease as production levels increase as the fixed costs are spread over more units. Therefore the constant figure of contribution per unit is more useful in the decision making process.

2 Break-even point $= \dfrac{£1,100,000}{£28-17}$

$= 100,000$ units

Margin of safety $= \dfrac{115,000-100,000}{115,000} \times 100$

$= 13\%$

3 Target profit units $= \dfrac{£540,000+300,000}{£83-65}$

$= 46,667$ units

4 Profit volume ratio $= \dfrac{£40-28}{£40}$

$= 30\%$

Target profit sales revenue $= \dfrac{£518,000+250,000}{0.3}$

$= £2,560,000$

**5 Identify the limiting factor**

Materials - at maximum demand

(4 x 20,000) + (5 x 25,000) + (3 x 8,000) = 229,000 kg

Labour hours - at maximum demand

(2 x 20,000) + (3 x 25,000) + (3 x 8,000) = 139,000 hours

Machine hours - at maximum demand

(4 x 20,000) + (3 x 25,000) + (2 x 8,000) = 171,000 hours

Therefore the only limiting factor is labour hours.

**Contribution per labour hour**

| | *R* | *S* | *T* |
|---|---|---|---|
| Contribution | £11 | £14 | £19 |
| Labour hours | 2 | 3 | 3 |
| Contribution per labour hour | £5.50 | £4.67 | £6.33 |
| Ranking | 2 | 3 | 1 |

**Production plan**

| | *Units* | *Labour hours used* | *Cumulative labour hours used* |
|---|---|---|---|
| T | 8,000 | 24,000 | 24,000 |
| R | 20,000 | 40,000 | 64,000 |
| S (balance) | 12,000 | 36,000 | 100,000 |
| | | 100,000 | |

**Contribution earned**

| | £ |
|---|---|
| R (20,000 x £11) | 220,000 |
| S (12,000 x £14) | 168,000 |
| T (8,000 x £19) | 152,000 |
| | 540,000 |

# answers to chapter 9: LONG TERM DECISION MAKING

1 The time value of money is the principle that a sum of money received now is worth more than the same sum received at some time in the future due to the fact that this sum could be invested now to earn interest. This means that a sum of money receivable or payable at some time in the future is worth less than its face value now due to the interest that is lost on not investing. Therefore future cash flows must be discounted in order to determine their present value.

2 a) **Payback period**

| | *Cash inflows* | *Cumulative cash inflows* |
|---|---|---|
| | £ | £ |
| 31 Dec 2003 | 15,000 | 15,000 |
| 31 Dec 2004 | 25,000 | 40,000 |
| 31 Dec 2005 | 35,000 | 75,000 |
| 31 Dec 2006 | 30,000 | 105,000 |

The payback period is 4 years if the cash flows are assumed to take place at the year end. Therefore the project should be rejected by the managers as it does not meet their payback criteria.

Even if the cash flows were assumed to occur evenly the payback period would still be more than three years.

b) **Net present value**

| *Time* | *Cash flow* | *Discount factor* | *Present value* |
|---|---|---|---|
| | £ | @ 10% | £ |
| 0 | (95,000) | 1.000 | (95,000) |
| 1 | 15,000 | 0.909 | 13,635 |
| 2 | 25,000 | 0.826 | 20,650 |
| 3 | 35,000 | 0.751 | 26,285 |
| 4 | 30,000 | 0.683 | 20,490 |
| 5 | 30,000 | 0.621 | 18,630 |
| Net present value | | | 4,690 |

As the project has a positive net present value then the managers should invest in the new plant and machinery as even after taking account of the time value of money the project shows a surplus.

c) In both calculations the cash flows have been assumed to occur at the end of the year.

d) The payback period investment criteria showed that the project should be rejected as the payback period method only considers the cash flows within the payback period limit. In fact in this case there are substantial cash flows later in this project's life. The net present value method takes account of all of the cash flows of the project and discounts each year's cash flows to take account of the time value of money. In this case the net present value is positive and therefore the investment is worthwhile even though it takes four years to payback the initial investment cost.

**3**

| | | | |
|---|---|---|---|
| i) | £24,000 x 0.873 | = | £20,952 |
| ii) | £1,500 x 2.402 | = | £3,603 |
| iii) | $\frac{£2,000}{0.06}$ | = | £33,333 |
| iv) | £30,000 x 1.000 | = | £30,000 |
| v) | £700 + (£700 x 3.546) | = | £3,182.20 |

**4 Net present value**

| *Time* | *Cash flow* £ | *Discount factor* *@ 7%* | *Present value* £ |
|---|---|---|---|
| 0 | (84,000) | 1.000 | (84,000) |
| 1 | 26,000 | 0.935 | 24,310 |
| 2 | 30,000 | 0.873 | 26,190 |
| 3 | 21,000 | 0.816 | 17,136 |
| 4 | 14,000 | 0.763 | 10,682 |
| Net present value | | | (5,682) |

On the basis of the net present value calculations, as the net present value of the business is negative, the directors should not purchase the sole trader's business.

**5 a) Net present value**

| *Time* | *Cash flow* £ | *Discount factor* *@ 12%* | *Present value* £ |
|---|---|---|---|
| 0 | (355,000) | 1.000 | (355,000) |
| 1 (47 + 60) | 107,000 | 0.893 | 95,551 |
| 2 (55 + 60) | 115,000 | 0.797 | 91,655 |
| 3 (68 + 60) | 128,000 | 0.712 | 91,136 |
| 4 (53 + 60) | 113,000 | 0.636 | 71,868 |
| 5 (22 + 60) | 82,000 | 0.567 | 46,494 |
| Net present value | | | 41,704 |

Note that depreciation is not a cash flow and having been charged in arriving at the profit figure must be added back to find the cash inflow in each year.

b) It has been assumed that the profit is earned on the last day of each year.

c) The net present value of the investment is positive and on this basis the potential investment is worthwhile.

**6** a) **Net present value at 15%**

| *Time* | *Cash flow* | *Discount factor* | *Present value* |
|---|---|---|---|
| | £ | *@ 15%* | £ |
| 0 | (84,000) | 1.000 | (84,000) |
| 0 | (180,000) | 1.000 | (180,000) |
| 1 | 42,000 | 0.870 | 36,540 |
| 2 | 50,000 | 0.756 | 37,800 |
| 3 | 75,000 | 0.658 | 49,350 |
| 4 | 80,000 | 0.572 | 45,760 |
| Net present value | | | (10,550) |

At the cost of capital of 15% the project has a negative net present value, and should therefore be rejected.

b) **Net present value at 10%**

| *Time* | *Cash flow* | *Discount factor* | *Present value* |
|---|---|---|---|
| | £ | *@ 10%* | £ |
| 0 | (180,000) | 1.000 | (180,000) |
| 1 | 42,000 | 0.909 | 38,178 |
| 2 | 50,000 | 0.826 | 41,300 |
| 3 | 75,000 | 0.751 | 56,325 |
| 4 | 80,000 | 0.683 | 54,640 |
| Net present value | | | 10,443 |

If the project can be financed at 10%, it should be accepted as it has a positive NPV.

c) The IRR is the discount rate or cost of capital at which the NPV of the project is zero. It tells a business the maximum discount rate at which the project is worthwhile.

# answers to chapter 10: INTERNAL INFORMATION

1 i) The factory supervisor will be concerned about the day to day operations of the factory employees. The type of information that he might require would include:

- schedules of production for each day/week in order to schedule the employees suitably
- details of employee's holidays in order to help to schedule the work
- details of absentees
- details of hours worked by each employee and in particular overtime hours
- whether production schedules are met
- requirements for any additional overtime

ii) The manufacturing director will be concerned more about the costs and overall performance of the labour force. The type of information that he might require would include:

- summaries of hours worked in each period including overtime hours
- the breakdown of overtime hours into week day and weekend overtime
- whether production targets have been met
- total labour cost in each period
- all variances from budget for the labour force

iii) The managing director will only really be concerned with any problem areas with the labour force. He will leave all other aspects to the factory supervisor and manufacturing director. The type of information that he might require would include:

- any significant labour variances from budget
- any excessive overtime worked
- any delays that have meant that production schedules have not been met

**2** The general requirements for useful information is that it must be relevant, reliable, consistent and prompt. Each of these will be considered in turn.

**Relevance** – Information will be relevant if it is information that that particular person requires - not all personnel in the organisation will require the same amount of detailed information. The more junior management will require details about the day to day running of their part of the organisation but further up the management levels less detailed information will be required -the relevant information for higher levels of management will be overviews, summaries, variances and problem areas.

**Reliable** – In order to be useful information must be reliable - this means that it must be as accurate as possible. Some information is factual, such as the number of hours of overtime worked in a week - this must be correct. Other information may be more subjective, such as the possible reasons for more materials being used in a period than was budgeted for - however again this should be as accurate as is possible given the circumstances.

**Consistent** – Information that is provided within an organisation will tend to be provided on a regular basis, weekly, monthly, quarterly etc and this information will often be compared over time. It is therefore important that each time the information is provided that it is provided on a consistent basis - the same format and with the same bases for all calculations, otherwise a comparison of one period's information to that of another would not be of use.

**Prompt** – When management require internal information about their business then they require it in order to be able to make decisions and to plan and control the business. In order to be able to do this the information that they require must be up to date. If figures for production in the factory for a week are required they will normally be required early in the following week not two or three weeks later.

**3** The typical type of information that might be required by the partners of a firm of solicitors in order to be able to appraise the performance of the firm for the last month might include:

- chargeable hours of all levels of staff
- amounts billed to clients during the month
- amounts of overtime worked by staff
- levels of overheads for the month
- potential new clients gained in the month
- absentee/illness rates
- amounts billed per chargeable hour

**4**

| | *Abberville* | *Bacup* | *Calver* | *Total* |
|---|---|---|---|---|
| | £ | £ | £ | £ |
| Sales | 137,489 | 195,374 | 104,328 | 437,191 |
| Cost of sales | 53,621 | 72,288 | 41,731 | 167,640 |
| Gross profit | 83,868 | 123,086 | 62,597 | 269,551 |
| Expenses | 33,373 | 37,121 | 22,952 | 93,446 |
| Net profit | 50,495 | 85,965 | 39,645 | 176,105 |

# answers to chapter 11: PERFORMANCE MEASURES

**1**

| | *Quarter ending 30 June 2003* | *Quarter ending 31 March 2003* |
|---|---|---|
| Cost per unit | $\frac{£567,900}{330,000}$ | $\frac{£580,400}{332,000}$ |
| | = £1.72 | = £1.75 |
| Labour productivity | $\frac{330,000}{12,600 \text{ hours}}$ | $\frac{332,000}{12,300}$ |
| | = 26.2 units per hour | 27 units per hour |
| Productivity index | $\frac{330,000}{350,000}$ | $\frac{332,000}{320,000}$ |
| | = 94.3% | = 103.8% |

**2**

**FACTORY**

Cost per unit $\frac{£557,800}{128,700}$ = £4.33 per unit

Labour productivity $\frac{128,700}{39,400}$ = 3.27 units per hour

Labour productivity $\frac{128,700}{280}$ = 460 units per employee

Productivity index $\frac{128,700}{120,000}$ = 107.3%

**TELEPHONE SALES**

Cost per order $\frac{£14,560}{9,180}$ = £1.59 per order

Labour productivity $\frac{9,180}{27}$ = 340 orders per person

3 Idle time is the time that the production workers are on the factory floor but are not actually producing the products of the organisation. Some idle time is necessary for Health and Safety reasons - workers must have time for coffee breaks, lunch breaks etc. This is known as unavoidable idle time as it is a necessary part of working life.

Other idle time however is a consequence of the manufacturing process. There may be bottlenecks in production which mean that some production workers are not able to work when they should. There may be machine breakdowns or a lack of materials that mean that there is no production to work on. The workers may have finished the assigned tasks for the day and no other task is available. This is all known as avoidable idle time as it is not strictly necessary although it is a practical aspect of factory life.

4

| | *Jan* | *Feb* | *Mar* | *Apr* | *May* | *June* |
|---|---|---|---|---|---|---|
| Labour utilisation % | $\frac{2,100}{2,190}$ | $\frac{2,050}{2,130}$ | $\frac{2,220}{2,240}$ | $\frac{2,200}{2,300}$ | $\frac{2,310}{2,430}$ | $\frac{2,250}{2,350}$ |
| | 95.9% | 96.2% | 99.1% | 95.7% | 95.1% | 95.7% |

5

| | *May* | *June* | *July* |
|---|---|---|---|
| Fixed asset utilisation | $\frac{£360,000}{£210,000}$ | $\frac{£402,000}{£190,000}$ | $\frac{£398,000}{£200,000}$ |
| | £1.71 | £2.11 | £1.99 |
| Machinery utilisation | $\frac{£360,000}{28,000 \text{ hours}}$ | $\frac{£402,000}{32,000 \text{ hours}}$ | $\frac{£398,000}{31,000 \text{ hours}}$ |
| | £12.86 per machine hour | £12.56 per machine hour | £12.84 per machine hour |
| Asset turnover | $\frac{£360,000}{£300,000}$ | $\frac{£402,000}{£310,000}$ | $\frac{£398,000}{£320,000}$ |
| | £1.20 | £1.30 | £1.24 |

**6**

| | May | June | July |
|---|---|---|---|
| Gross profit margin | $\frac{530}{1,320}$ | $\frac{570}{1,420}$ | $\frac{530}{1,500}$ |
| | 40.2% | 40.1% | 35.3% |
| Net profit margin | $\frac{240}{1,320}$ | $\frac{240}{1,420}$ | $\frac{240}{1,500}$ |
| | 18.2% | 16.9% | 16.0% |
| ROCE | $\frac{240}{2,600}$ | $\frac{240}{2,840}$ | $\frac{240}{3,080}$ |
| | 9.2% | 8.5% | 7.8% |

The gross profit margin has shown a significant decrease in July. The net profit margin decreased in June even though the gross profit margin was similar to that of May indicating an increase in expenses. The net profit margin again decreases in July largely due to the deteriorating gross profit margin.

The return on capital employed has decreased each month due to a combination of the gross and net profit margin decreases.

**7**

| | May | June | July |
|---|---|---|---|
| i) Cost per unit | $\frac{£416,000}{220,000}$ | $\frac{£402,000}{215,000}$ | $\frac{£403,000}{216,000}$ |
| | 1.89 | £1.87 | £1.87 |
| ii) Labour productivity | $\frac{220,000}{1,400}$ | $\frac{£215,000}{1,360}$ | $\frac{216,000}{1,430}$ |
| | 157 per hour | 158 per hour | 151 per hour |
| iii) Productivity index | $\frac{220,000}{220,000}$ | $\frac{215,000}{220,000}$ | $\frac{216,000}{220,000}$ |
| | 100% | 97.7% | 98.2% |
| iv) Labour utilisation % | $\frac{1,400}{1,400}$ | $\frac{1,360}{1,400}$ | $\frac{1,430}{1,400}$ |
| | 100% | 97.1% | 102.1% |

| | | | | |
|---|---|---|---|---|
| v) | Fixed asset utilisation | £595,000 / £320,000 | £600,000 / £300,000 | £610,000 / 340,000 |
| | | £1.86 | £2.00 | £1.79 |
| vi) | Asset turnover | £595,000 / 460,000 | £600,000 / £508,000 | £610,000 / £562,000 |
| | | £1.29 | £1.18 | £1.09 |
| vii) | Gross profit margin | £179,000 / 595,000 | £198,000 / £600,000 | £207,000 / £610,000 |
| | | 30.1% | 33.0% | 33.9% |
| viii) | Net profit margin | £48,000 / £595,000 | £54,000 / 600,000 | £58,000 / 610,000 |
| | | 8.1% | 9.0% | 9.5% |
| ix) | ROCE | £48,000 / 460,000 | £54,000 / 508,000 | £58,000 / 562,000 |
| | | 10.4% | 10.6% | 10.3% |

There have been few major changes over the three month period although perhaps the most notable is the increase in gross profit margin in June and July. This has led to an increased net profit margin in those months although no increase in return on capital employed.

On the whole the performance in June and July has not been as good as in May although one area of improvement is the decrease in the cost per unit in the last two months. However in July labour productivity decreased even though the labour utilisation level was good. However both fixed asset utilisation and asset turnover decreased contributing to the decrease in return on capital employed in July.

# answers to chapter 12: WRITING A REPORT

1
- Title of the report
- Who the report is from and to
- Date
- Terms of reference
- Summary
- Main body of the report
- Conclusion
- Recommendations
- Appendix

2

## REPORT

**To:** Sales Director
**From:** Accountant
**Date:** 19 August 2003
**Subject:** Shop Profitability

**Terms of reference**

This report on the profitability of the shop for the last six months has been requested by the sales director. A number of performance measures for profitability have been calculated and are shown in the appendix to this report.

**Summary**

The performance measures indicate not only a substantial increase in sales over the first six months of the year but also a healthy increase in all areas of profitability.

**Findings**

The major change in the shop performance has been a 50% increase in turnover in the six month period from January to June 2001. However this appears to have been achieved with an increase in profitability as well.

The gross profit margin has increased gradually each month from 40.9% in January to 45.2% in June. The net profit margin has also increased over the period from 14.8% to highs of 15.5% although there was a sharp decrease in March and April. This may have been due to costs incurred as part of the expansion such as advertising costs which then reverted to normal levels in later months.

The return on capital employed has largely followed the pattern of the net profit margin although over the period has shown a healthy increase from 9.4% to 10.6%. This increase has been helped by an increased asset turnover, or capital utilisation, which has leapt from 64 pence of sales per £1 of capital to 70 pence in June.

**Conclusion**

All profitability performance measures show a significant increase over the period combined with a large increase in turnover over the six months.

**APPENDIX**

**Performance measures**

| | *Jan* | *Feb* | *Mar* | *Apr* | *May* | *June* |
|---|---|---|---|---|---|---|
| Gross profit margin | 40.9% | 42.0% | 43.0% | 43.6% | 44.0% | 45.2% |
| Net profit margin | 14.8% | 15.5% | 14.0% | 14.5% | 15.5% | 15.1% |
| Return on capital employed | 9.4% | 9.7% | 9.0% | 9.9% | 10.7% | 10.6% |
| Asset turnover | 0.64 | 0.63 | 0.64 | 0.68 | 0.69 | 0.70 |

3

# REPORT

**To:** Manufacturing director
**From:** Accountant
**Date:** 20 July 2003
**Subject:** Productivity of divisions

**Terms of reference**

This report on productivity in each of the three manufacturing divisions has been prepared for the manufacturing director. The findings of the report are based upon the performance measures shown in the appendix to this report.

**Summary**

There are no significant differences between the performance of the three divisions although on the whole the most productive division is Division B and the least productive Division A. The most concerning factor is probably the fact that both units produced and hours worked are below budget in all three divisions.

**Findings**

The cost per unit figures do not differ significantly between the three divisions although the range is £3.12 to £3.05 in Division C. If all three divisions could produce the products at a cost of £3.05 this would clearly help the profitability of the organisation as a whole.

The productivity per labour hour again shows no huge differences but only Division B has achieved the budgeted productivity of 30 units per labour hour.

The productivity index shows that all of the Divisions have produced less than the units that were budgeted for. In line with this the labour utilisation figures show that less hours were worked than were budgeted for. This may need to be investigated.

Of the three Divisions, Division B appears to have performed the best with a fairly low cost per unit together with budgeted productivity per hour and the best performance in terms of productivity index and labour utilisation. Division A appears to have performed less well than the other two divisions with all performance measures being lower.

**Conclusion**

There are no dramatic differences in the performance of the three divisions although on balance Division B appears to be the most productive and Division A the least.

**APPENDIX**

**Performance measures**

| | *Division A* | *Division B* | *Division C* |
|---|---|---|---|
| Cost per unit | £3.12 | £3.08 | £3.05 |
| Productivity per labour hour | 28.6 | 30.0 | 28.8 |
| Productivity index | 88.9% | 96.0% | 90.9% |
| Labour utilisation | 93.3% | 96.0% | 94.5% |

# answers to chapter 13: TABLES AND DIAGRAMS

1 a)

| | A | B | C | D | E |
|---|---|---|---|---|---|
| 1 | | June | July | August | September |
| 2 | Sales | 48,700 | 50,200 | 45,600 | 46,800 |
| 3 | Cost of sales | 30,200 | 31,600 | 29,200 | 30,000 |
| 4 | Gross profit | = B2 - B3 | = C2 - C3 | = D2 - D3 | = E2 - E3 |
| 5 | Expenses | 12,200 | 12,500 | 11,400 | 11,700 |
| 6 | Net profit | = B4 - B5 | = C4 - C5 | = D4 - D5 | = E4 - E5 |
| 7 | Capital | 52,500 | 52,500 | 55,000 | 55,000 |
| 8 | Gross profit % | =(B4/B2)*100 | =(C4/C2)*100 | =(D4/D2)*100 | =(E4/E2)*100 |
| 9 | Net profit % | =(B6/B2)*100 | =(C6/C2)*100 | =(D6/D2)*100 | =(E6/E2)*100 |
| 10 | ROCE | =(B6/B7)*100 | =(C6/C7)*100 | =(D6/D7)*100 | =(E6/E7)*100 |
| 11 | Asset turnover | =B2/B7 | =C2/C7 | =D4/D7 | =E4/E7 |

b)

| | A | B | C | D | E |
|---|---|---|---|---|---|
| 1 | | June | July | August | September |
| 2 | Sales | 48,700 | 50,200 | 45,600 | 46,800 |
| 3 | Cost of sales | 30,200 | 31,600 | 29,200 | 30,000 |
| 4 | Gross profit | 18,500 | 18,600 | 16,400 | 16,800 |
| 5 | Expenses | 12,200 | 12,500 | 11,400 | 11,700 |
| 6 | Net profit | 6,300 | 6,100 | 5,000 | 5,100 |
| 7 | Capital | 52,500 | 52,500 | 55,000 | 55,000 |
| 8 | Gross profit % | 38.0 | 37.1 | 36.0 | 35.9 |
| 9 | Net profit % | 12.9 | 12.2 | 11.0 | 10.9 |
| 10 | ROCE | 12.0 | 11.6 | 9.1 | 9.3 |
| 11 | Asset turnover | 0.93 | 0.96 | 0.83 | 0.85 |

**2**

| | A | B | C |
|---|---|---|---|
| 1 | | Quarter ending 30/3 | Quarter ending 30/6 |
| 2 | Budgeted production | 320,000 | 350,000 |
| 3 | Actual production | 332,000 | 330,000 |
| 4 | Production cost | £580,400 | £567,900 |
| 5 | Hours worked | 12,300 | 12,600 |
| 6 | Cost per unit | =B4/B3 | =C4/C3 |
| 7 | Labour productivity | =B3/B5 | =C3/C5 |
| 8 | Productivity index | =(B3/B2)*100 | =(C3/C2)*100 |

**3 MONTHLY SALES FIGURES**

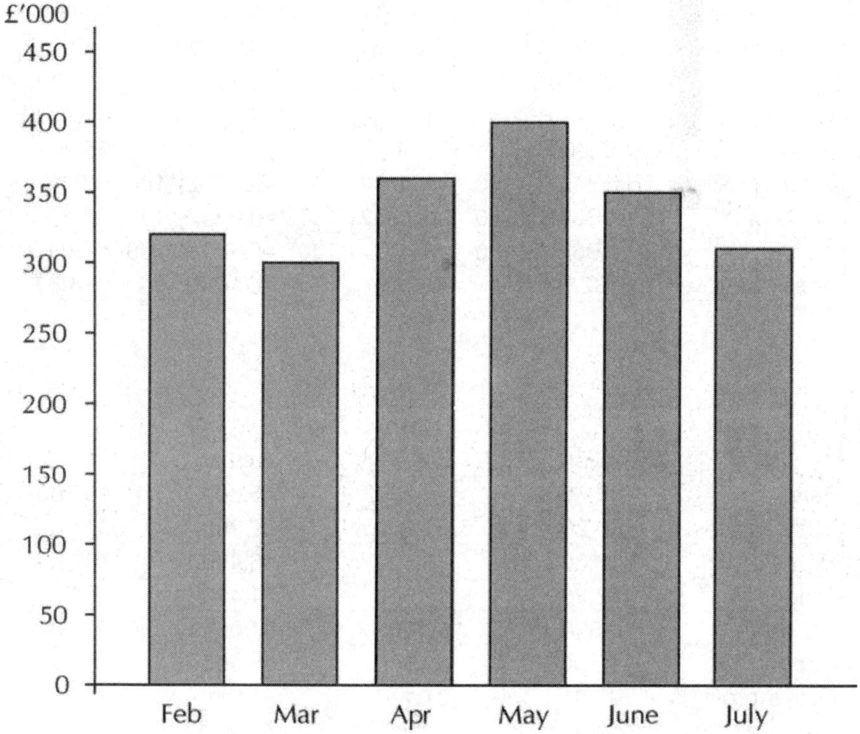

**4 SALES, GROSS PROFIT, NET PROFIT**

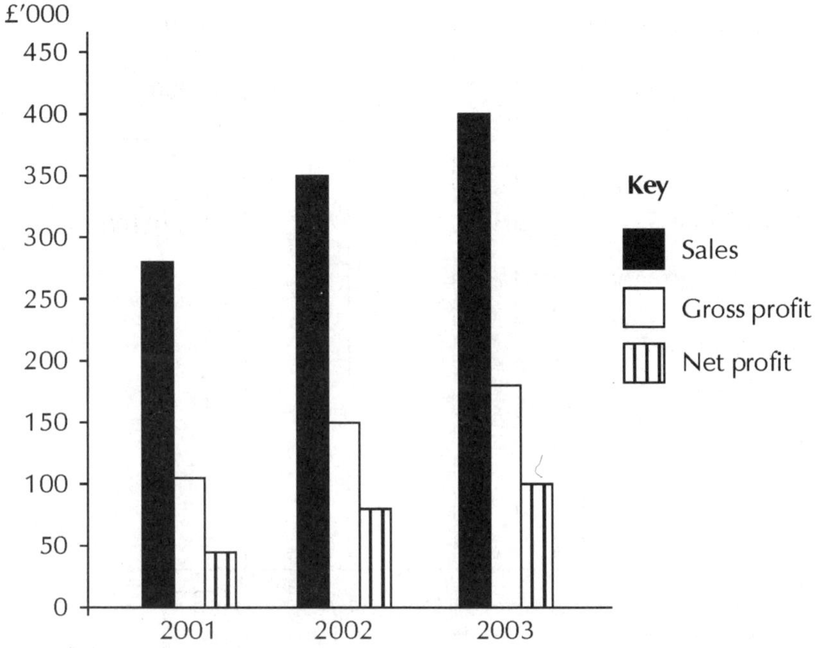

## 5 DIVISIONAL SALES

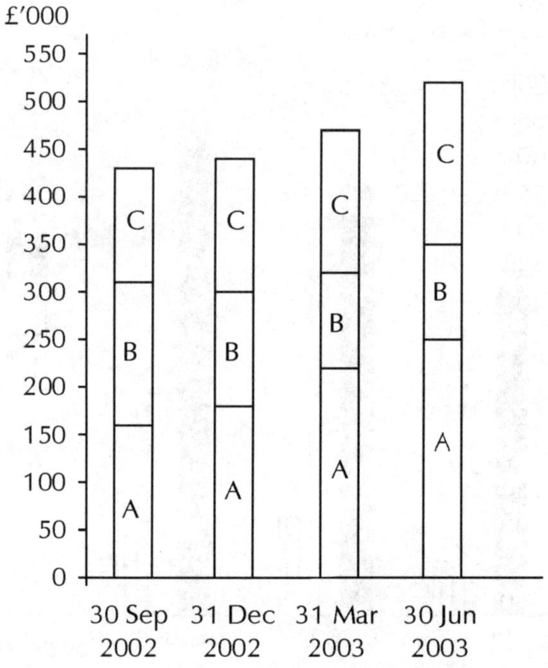

**6 i) TOTAL PROFIT**

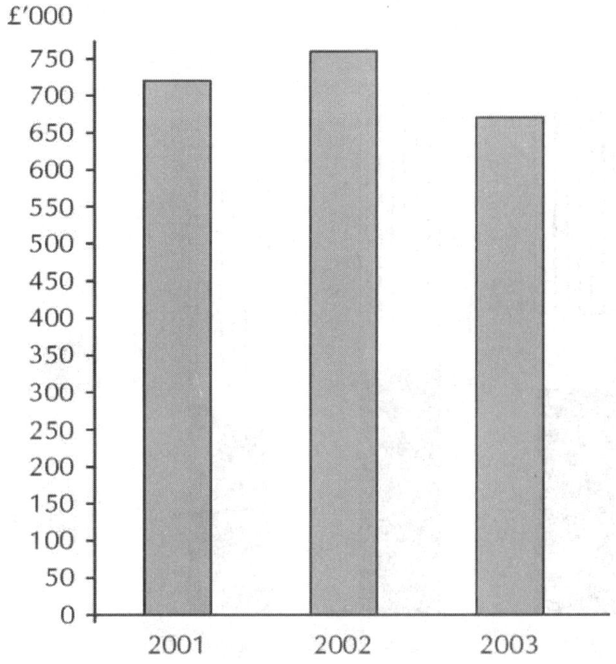


**ii) PROFIT BREAKDOWN**

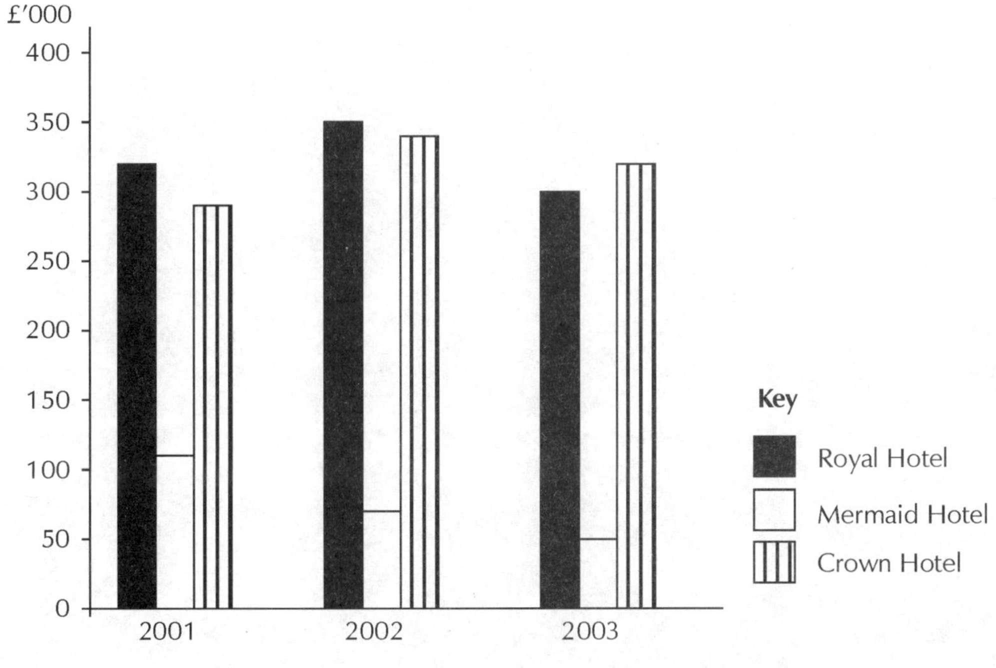

**iii) PROFIT BREAKDOWN**

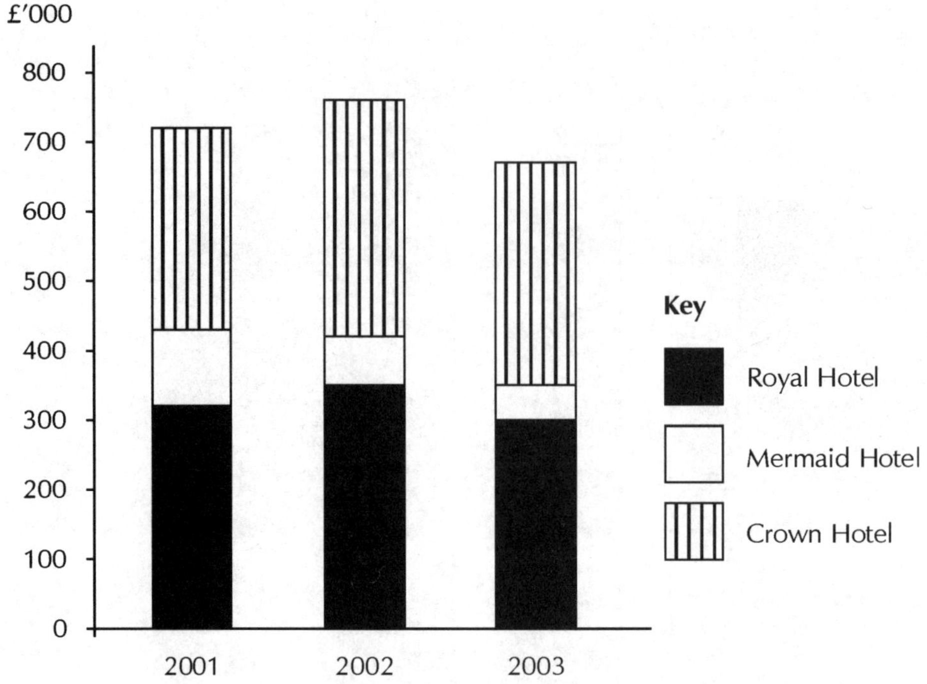

**7 TOTAL COSTS**

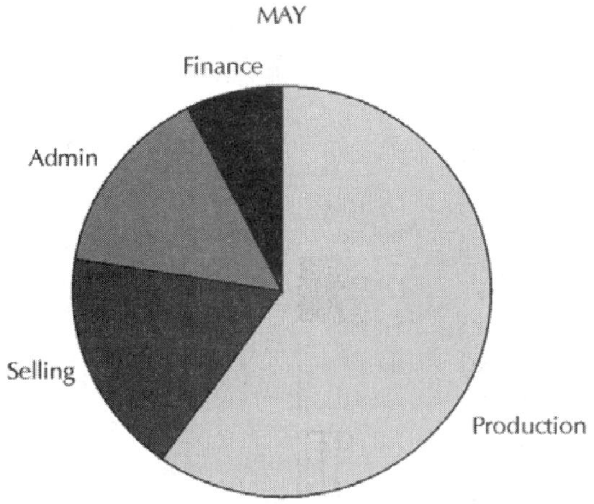


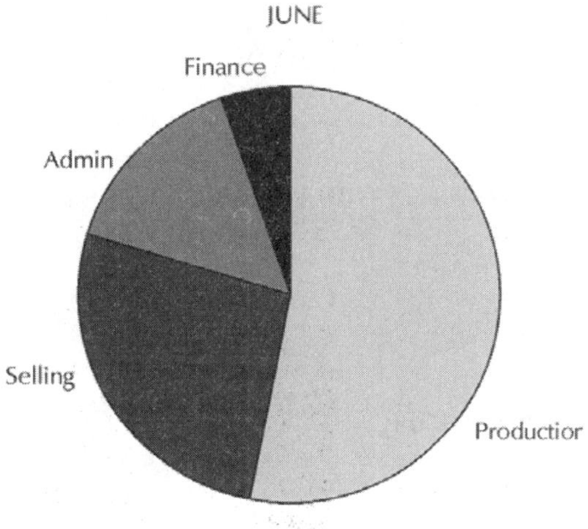


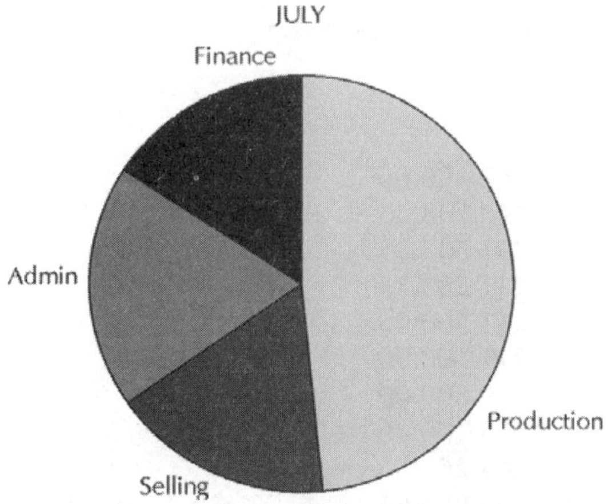

# answers to chapter 14: REPORTING FIGURES OVER TIME

**1** $$\frac{159+62+55+86+104+168+192}{7}$$

$$= \frac{826}{7}$$

= **118 per day**

**2**

| | £ | *3 month moving average* £ |
|---|---|---|
| July 2002 | 337,600 | |
| August 2002 | 415,300 | 347,466.66 |
| September 2002 | 289,500 | 323,733.33 |
| October 2002 | 266,400 | 251,533.33 |
| November 2002 | 198,700 | 241,233.33 |
| December 2002 | 258,600 | 211,500.00 |
| January 2003 | 177,200 | 211,700.00 |
| February 2003 | 199,300 | 199,800.00 |
| March 2003 | 222,900 | 226,100.00 |
| April 2003 | 256,100 | 248,266.66 |
| May 2003 | 265,800 | 295,866.66 |
| June 2003 | 365,700 | |

**3**

| *Week* | *Costs* | *4 week moving average* |
|---|---|---|
| | £ | £ |
| 1 | 128,500 | |
| 2 | 195,400 | |
| | | 162,575 |
| 3 | 148,600 | |
| | | 164,825 |
| 4 | 177,800 | |
| | | 157,400 |
| 5 | 137,500 | |
| | | 157,300 |
| 6 | 165,700 | |
| | | 158,700 |
| 7 | 148,200 | |
| | | 168,650 |
| 8 | 183,400 | |
| | | 168,400 |
| 9 | 177,300 | |
| | | 170,200 |
| 10 | 164,700 | |
| | | 172,750 |
| 11 | 155,400 | |
| | | 167,950 |
| 12 | 193,600 | |
| | | 170,400 |
| 13 | 158,100 | |
| | | 172,275 |
| 14 | 174,500 | |
| | | 163,725 |
| 15 | 162,900 | |
| 16 | 159,400 | |

**4**

| | A | B | C | D |
|---|---|---|---|---|
| 1 | Week 1 | 128,500 | | |
| 2 | | | | |
| 3 | Week 2 | 195,400 | | |
| 4 | | | =(B1+B3+B5+B7)/4 | |
| 5 | Week 3 | 148,600 | | =(C4+C6)/2 |
| 6 | | | =(B3+B5+B7+B9)/4 | |
| 7 | Week 4 | 177,800 | | =(C6+C8)/2 |
| 8 | | | =(B5+B7+B9+B11)/4 | |
| 9 | Week 5 | 137,500 | | =(C8+C10)/2 |
| 10 | | | =(B7+B9+B11+B13)/4 | |
| 11 | Week 6 | 165,700 | | =(C10+C12)/2 |
| 12 | | | =(B9+B11+B13+B15)/4 | |
| 13 | Week 7 | 148,200 | | =(C12+C14)/2 |
| 14 | | | =(B11+B13+B15+B17)/4 | |
| 15 | Week 8 | 183,400 | | =(C14+C16)/2 |
| 16 | | | =(B13+B15+B17+B19)/4 | |
| 17 | Week 9 | 177,300 | | =(C16+C18)/2 |
| 18 | | | =(B15+B17+B19+B21)/4 | |
| 19 | Week 10 | 164,700 | | =(C18+C20)/2 |
| 20 | | | =(B17+B19+B21+B23)/4 | |
| 21 | Week 11 | 155,400 | | =(C20+C22)/2 |
| 22 | | | =(B19+B21+B23+B25)/4 | |
| 23 | Week 12 | 193,600 | | =(C22+C24)/2 |
| 24 | | | =(B21+B23+B25+B27)/4 | |
| 25 | Week 13 | 158,100 | | =(C24+C26)/2 |
| 26 | | | =(B23+B25+B27+B29)/4 | |
| 27 | Week 14 | 174,500 | | =(C26+C28)/2 |
| 28 | | | =(B25+B27+B29+B31)/4 | |
| 29 | Week 15 | 162,900 | | |
| 30 | | | | |
| 31 | Week 16 | 159,400 | | |

**5** i)

| *2002* | £ | *3 month moving average* £ |
|---|---|---|
| January | 55,600 | |
| February | 52,700 | 54,800.00 |
| March | 56,100 | 55,200.00 |
| April | 56,800 | 57,066.67 |
| May | 58,300 | 58,533.33 |
| June | 60,500 | 59,233.33 |
| July | 58,900 | 59,533.33 |
| August | 59,200 | 59,800.00 |
| September | 61,300 | 60,866.67 |
| October | 62,100 | 62,266.67 |
| November | 63,400 | 62,733.33 |
| December | 62,700 | 62,466.67 |
| *2003* | | |
| January | 61,300 | 62,166.67 |
| February | 62,500 | 62,633.33 |
| March | 64,100 | 63,933.33 |
| April | 65,200 | 64,733.33 |
| May | 64,900 | 65,600.00 |
| June | 66,700 | |

ii) **MONTHLY SALES AND TREND**

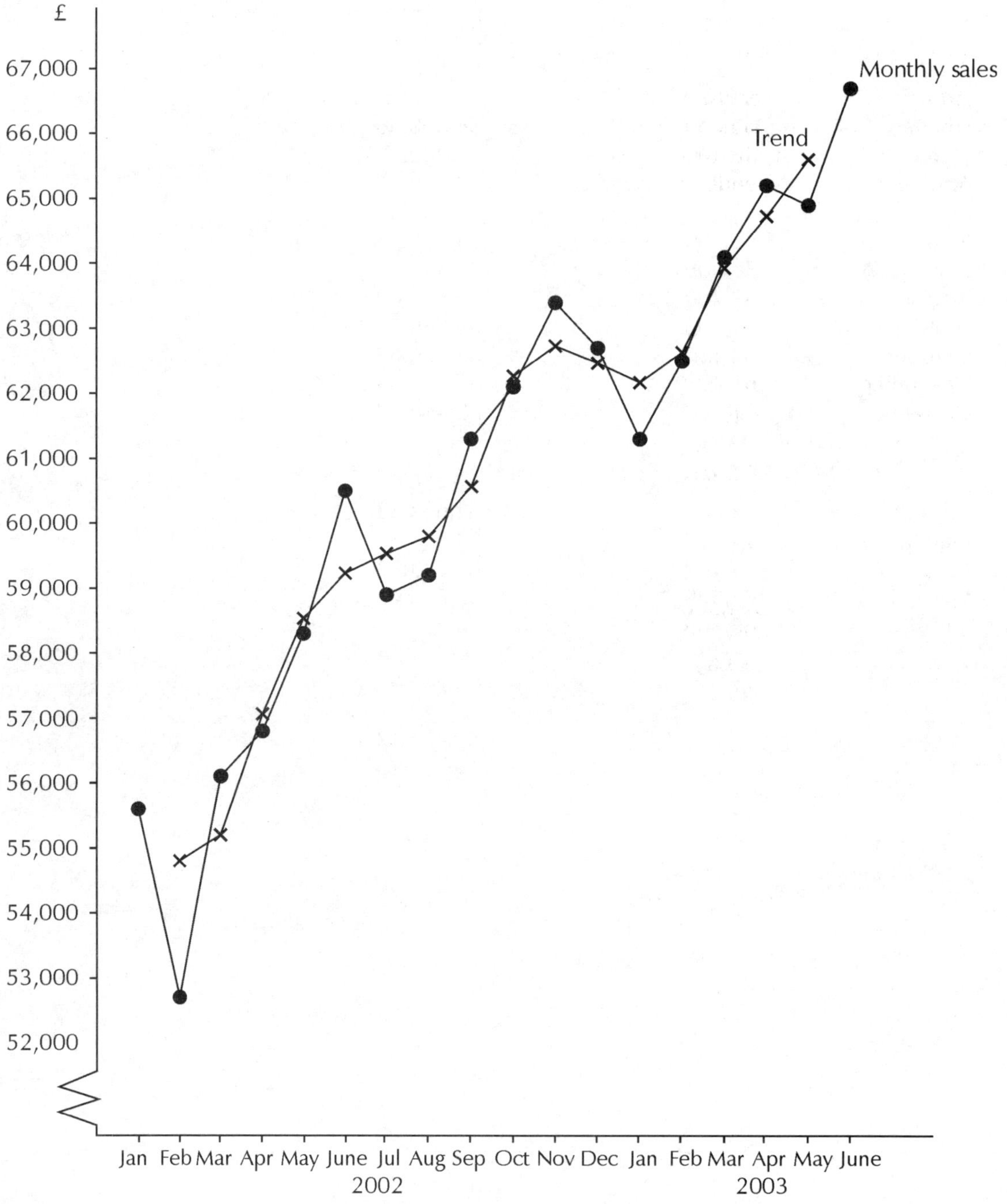

**6** Interpolation is a method of estimating a figure within a range of figures already available. Therefore if the costs of production for a factory range from £126,700 for 30,000 units to £193,500 for 40,000 units then if an estimate were required for the production cost of 37,500 units this could be found from a graph of these costs by reading off the anticipated cost figure for 37,500 units.

Extrapolation however is a method of estimating a figure that is outside the range of figures already available. Using the same production cost example, if an estimate was required for the production cost of 45,000 units then the graph line would have to be extended and the estimated cost figure read off from the extended graph.

**7**

| *2002* | £ | | *Index* |
|---|---|---|---|
| August | 527,500 | | 100.00 |
| September | 513,400 | 513,400/527,500 x 100 | 97.33 |
| October | 556,700 | 556,700/527,500 x 100 | 105.54 |
| November | 523,400 | 523,400/527,500 x 100 | 99.22 |
| December | 582,300 | 582,300/527,500 x 100 | 110.39 |
| *2003* | | | |
| January | 561,300 | 561,300/527,500 x 100 | 106.41 |
| February | 532,600 | 532,600/527,500 x 100 | 100.97 |
| March | 524,300 | 524,300/527,500 x 100 | 99.39 |
| April | 515,700 | 515,700/527,500 x 100 | 97.76 |
| May | 529,600 | 529,600/527,500 x 100 | 100.40 |
| June | 538,200 | 538,200/527,500 x 100 | 102.03 |

**8** a) RPI adjusted sales

| | | |
|---|---|---|
| January | | 162,400 |
| February | 163,800 x 171.1/172.0 | 162,943 |
| March | 165,900 x 171.1/172.2 | 164,840 |
| April | 167,200 x 171.1/173.0 | 165,364 |
| May | 166,200 x 171.1/172.1 | 165,234 |
| June | 164,100 x 171.1/171.3 | 163,908 |
| July | 162,300 x 171.1/171.0 | 162,395 |
| August | 160,500 x 171.1/170.3 | 161,254 |

b) Index

| | | |
|---|---|---|
| January | | 100.0 |
| February | 162,943/162.400 x 100 | 100.3 |
| March | 164,840/162.400 x 100 | 101.5 |
| April | 165,364/162,400 x 100 | 101.8 |
| May | 165,234/162,400 x 100 | 101.7 |
| June | 163,908/162,400 x 100 | 100.9 |
| July | 162,395/162,400 x 100 | 100.0 |
| August | 161,254/162,400 x 100 | 99.3 |

c)

| | A | B | C | D | E |
|---|---|---|---|---|---|
| 1 | January | 162,400 | 171.1 | =B1*(C1/C1) | =(D1/D1)*100 |
| 2 | February | 163,800 | 172.0 | =B2*(C1/C2) | =(D2/D1)*100 |
| 3 | March | 165,900 | 172.2 | =B3*(C1/C3) | =(D3/D1)*100 |
| 4 | April | 167,200 | 173.0 | =B4*(C1/C4) | =(D4/D1)*100 |
| 5 | May | 166,200 | 172.1 | =B5*(C1/C5) | =(D5/D1)*100 |
| 6 | June | 164,100 | 171.3 | =B6*(C1/C6) | =(D6/D1)*100 |
| 7 | July | 162,300 | 171.0 | =B7*(C1/C7) | =(D7/D1)*100 |
| 8 | August | 160,500 | 170.3 | =B8*(C1/C8) | =(D8/D1)*100 |

# answers to chapter 15: EXTERNAL REPORTING

1 The National Statistics 'themes' are:

- agriculture, fishing and forestry
- commerce, energy and industry
- compendia and reference
- crime and justice
- economy
- education and training
- health and care
- labour market
- national and built environment
- population and migration
- social and welfare
- transport, travel and tourism
- other

**2**

# BARDEN LOCAL DISTRICT COUNCIL
# GRANT APPLICATION

## PART 1 BUSINESS DETAILS

Business name ....D.&.G Harper..............................................

.........................................................................

Business address ...Harper.House............................................

.................East Park Road..............................................

.................Barden.BD4.6GK.............................................

Business telephone .02185 3743..............................................

Business fax ......02185 3264...............................................

Owner's name .....David and Gareth Harper...................................

.........................................................................

Type of business ...Curtain and blind manufacturer...........................

.........................................................................

.........................................................................

.........................................................................

## PART 2 FINANCIAL DETAILS

### 2A TURNOVER AND PROFIT

Figures are to be provided for annual turnover and reported net profit for the last three complete financial years

| Financial year ended: | | UK turnover £ | Export turnover £ | Net profit £ |
|---|---|---|---|---|
| Month | Year | | | |
| June | 2001 | 378,690 | 10,580 | 74,110 |
| June | 2002 | 735,400 | 38,600 | 162,540 |
| June | 2003 | 882,400 | 48,340 | 204,770 |

### 2B WORKING CAPITAL

Figures are to be provided for working capital at the end of the most recent financial year.

Year ending: 30 June 2003

| | £ |
|---|---|
| Current assets | 97,470 |
| Minus: current liabilities | (42,170) |
| Working capital | 55,300 |

### 2C FIXED ASSETS

Figures are to be provided for fixed asset totals at the end of the most recent financial year.

Year ending: 30 June 2003

| | £ |
|---|---|
| Land and buildings | 184,500 |
| Plant and machinery | 190,400 |
| Other | 97,700 |
| Total fixed assets | 472,600 |

## PART 3 NON FINANCIAL DETAILS

### 3A EMPLOYMENT DETAILS

Figures are to be provided for the number of employees for the last three financial years.

| Financial year ended: | | Number of full time employees | Number of part time employees |
|---|---|---|---|
| Month | Year | | |
| June | 2001 | 9 | 1 |
| June | 2002 | 14 | 3 |
| June | 2003 | 14 | 3 |

### 3B BUSINESS DETAILS

Date business started: 1994

Business type -

- Sole trader ☐
- Partnership ☑
- Company ☐

## PART 4 GRANT APPLICATION

Indicate in the space provided the reasons for the grant application. If the grant application is processed further more detail will be requested at a later date.

Grant application for £15,000 to help fund additional factory space and potential employment of 6 additional full time employees.

**3**

# CHAMBER OF COMMERCE
# ANNUAL ECONOMIC REVIEW

Please tick the appropriate box in answer to each question - all answers will be treated in the strictest confidence. All answers should be based upon the business performance for the last full financial year.

## 1 BUSINESS DETAILS

End of last full financial year:

Turnover range:

| | |
|---|---|
| Upto £50,000 | ☐ |
| £50,000 - £100,000 | ☐ |
| £100,000 - £250,000 | ☐ |
| £250,000 - £500,000 | ☑ |
| £500,000 - £1,000,000 | ☐ |
| Over £1,000,000 | ☐ |

Main business activity:

| | | | |
|---|---|---|---|
| Engineering | ☐ | Health | ☐ |
| Construction | ☑ | Art and design | ☐ |
| Agriculture | ☐ | Transport | ☐ |
| Energy | ☐ | Tourism | ☐ |
| Retail | ☐ | Other (please state) ......... | |
| Education | ☐ | ......................... | |

**2 TURNOVER**

Percentage of total turnover accounted for by export sales:

| | | | |
|---|---|---|---|
| 0% | ☑ | 30% to 50% | ☐ |
| upto 10% | ☐ | 50% to 75% | ☐ |
| 10% to 20% | ☐ | 75% to 100% | ☐ |
| 20% to 30% | ☐ | | |

Percentage increase/decrease in turnover compared to previous financial year:

| | | | |
|---|---|---|---|
| Decrease upto 20% | ☐ | Increase upto 20% | ☐ |
| Decrease of 20% to 50% | ☐ | Increase of 20% to 50% | ☑ |
| Decrease of more than 50% | ☐ | Increase of more than 50% | ☐ |

Percentage increase/decrease in net profit compared to previous financial year:

| | | | |
|---|---|---|---|
| Decrease upto 20% | ☐ | Increase upto 20% | ☐ |
| Decrease of 20% to 50% | ☐ | Increase of 20% to 50% | ☑ |
| Decrease of more than 50% | ☐ | Increase of more than 50% | ☐ |

**3 BUSINESS CONFIDENCE**

Do you consider that over the following 12 months:

| | | | | | |
|---|---|---|---|---|---|
| Turnover | will increase | ☑ | Profitability | will increase | ☑ |
| | remain the same | ☐ | | remain the same | ☐ |
| | decrease | ☐ | | decrease | ☐ |

# answers to chapter 16: VALUE ADDED TAX

**1** i) From 1 April 2004 the VAT registration threshold is **£58,000**

ii) From 1 April 2004 the VAT deregistration limit is **£56,000**

iii) VAT on purchases is known as **input** tax

iv) VAT on sales is known as **output** tax

v) A VAT return is normally completed every **3** months

**2** Standard rate of 17.5%

Reduced rate of 5% on domestic fuel

Zero rate 0%

**3** i) £15,862.50 - as a business making exempt supplies cannot reclaim any input VAT

ii) £13,500.00 - as a business making zero-rated supplies can reclaim input VAT

**4** If the business makes zero-rated supplies then it will not have to pay VAT over to Customs and Excise but as a VAT registered business will be able to reclaim any input VAT suffered.

**5** i) £16,685.00 – the VAT on cars for use in a business is not reclaimable

ii) £141.00 – the VAT on business entertaining is not reclaimable

**6** i) 13 August 2003 – actual tax point

ii) 15 August 2003 – basic tax point

iii) 12 August 2003 – actual tax point

iv) 20 August 2003 – actual tax point

**7** i) £25.69

ii) £34.65

iii) £33.95

iv) £43.90

**8** i) VAT £64.36
Net of VAT £367.80

ii) VAT £39.13
Net of VAT £223.64

iii) VAT £32.30
Net of VAT £184.60

iv) VAT £46.19
Net of VAT £263.99

**9**
- The business name, address and VAT registration number
- The date of supply
- Description of goods/services
- For each applicable VAT rate the total including VAT and the VAT rate

# answers to chapter 17: VAT RECORDS

1

**VAT account**

| **VAT deductible – input tax** | **£** | **VAT payable – output tax** | **£** |
|---|---|---|---|
| Purchases day book | 2,485.61 | Sales day book | 3,474.89 |
| Cash payments book | 624.78 | Cash receipts book | 993.57 |
| EU acquisitions | 925.47 | EU acquisitions | 925.47 |
| | 4,035.86 | | 5,393.93 |
| Less: credit notes received | 210.68 | Less: credit notes issued | 441.46 |
| Total VAT deductible | 3,825.18 | Total VAT payable | 4,952.47 |
| | | Less: VAT deductible | 3,825.18 |
| | | Due to Customs & Excise | 1,127.29 |

2

**VAT account**

| **VAT deductible – input tax** | **£** | **VAT payable – output tax** | **£** |
|---|---|---|---|
| Purchases day book | 4,668.14 | Sales day book | 6,275.78 |
| Cash payments book | 936.47 | Cash receipts book | 1,447.30 |
| EU acquisitions | 772.46 | EU acquisitions | 772.46 |
| Bad debt relief | 284.67 | | |
| Net overcharge for previous period (221.68 – 126.57) | 95.11 | | |
| | 6,756.85 | | 8,495.54 |
| Less: credit notes received | 510.36 | Less: credit notes issued | 726.58 |
| Total VAT deductible | 6,246.49 | Total VAT payable | 7,768.96 |
| | | Less: VAT deductible | 6,246.49 |
| | | Due to Customs & Excise | 1,522.47 |

**3**

## Value Added Tax Return

For the period
to

For Official Use

Registration number: 234 4576 12

Period: 02 03

You could be liable to a financial penalty if your completed return and all the VAT payable are not received by the due date.

**Waltzer Enterprises**
**Adam Industrial Park**
**Yarden**
**LR3 9GS**

Due date: 31 July 2003

For Official Use

Your VAT Office telephone number is 0123-4567

Before you fill in this form please read the notes on the back and the VAT Leaflet *"Filling in your VAT return"*. Fill in all boxes clearly in ink, and write 'none' where necessary. Don't put a dash or leave any box blank. If there are no pence write "00" in the pence column. Do not enter more than one amount in any box.

For official use

| | Box | £ | p |
|---|---|---|---|
| VAT due in this period on sales and other outputs | 1 | 10,177 | 80 |
| VAT due in this period on acquisitions from other EC Member States | 2 | 275 | 17 |
| Total VAT due (the sum of boxes 1 and 2) | 3 | 10,452 | 97 |
| VAT reclaimed in this period on purchases and other inputs (including acquisitions from the EC) | 4 | 6,163 | 12 |
| Net VAT to be paid to Customs or reclaimed by you (Difference between boxes 3 and 4) | 5 | 4,289 | 85 |
| Total value of sales and all other outputs excluding any VAT. Include your box 8 figure | 6 | 61,551 | 00 |
| Total value of purchases and all other inputs excluding any VAT. Include your box 9 figure | 7 | 37,729 | 00 |
| Total value of all supplies of goods and related services, excluding any VAT, to other EC Member States | 8 | NONE | 00 |
| Total value of all acquisitions of goods and related services, excluding any VAT, from other EC Member States | 9 | 1,572 | 00 |

**Retail schemes.** If you have used any ot the schemes in the period covered by this return, enter the relevant letter(s) in this box.

If you are enclosing a payment please tick this box. ☑

DECLARATION: You, or someone on your behalf, must sign below.

I, .................................................................................... declare that the
(Full name of signatory in BLOCK LETTERS)
information given above is true and complete.

Signature.......................................................... Date ............. 20

**A false declaration can result in prosecution.**

**B**

## 3 WORKINGS

| | | £ |
|---|---|---|
| Box 1 | Sales day book | 10,082.76 |
| | Cash receipts book | 931.98 |
| | Sales returns day book | (836.94) |
| | | 10,177.80 |
| | | |
| Box 4 | Purchases day book – EU | 275.17 |
| | Purchases day book – UK | 5,892.69 |
| | Cash payments book | 552.55 |
| | Purchases returns day book | (557.29) |
| | | 6,163.12 |
| | | |
| Box 6 | Sales day book – zero rated | 3,628.47 |
| | Sales day book – standard | 57,615.80 |
| | Cash receipts book | 5,325.65 |
| | Sales returns day book – zero | (236.34) |
| | Sales returns – standard | (4,782.57) |
| | | 61,551.01 |
| | | |
| Box 7 | Purchases day book – EU | 1,572.45 |
| | Purchases day book – zero | 2,636.47 |
| | Purchases day book – standard | 33,672.57 |
| | Cash payments book | 3,157.46 |
| | Purchases returns – zero | (125.34) |
| | Purchases returns – standard | (3,184.57) |
| | | 37,729.04 |

**4** If a net error of more than £2,000 is discovered then this cannot be adjusted for on the VAT return. Instead voluntary disclosure must be made to the local VAT Business Advice Centre using Form VAT 652 or in a letter.

**5** If you have been registered for VAT for at least 12 months and the annual value of your taxable supplies, excluding VAT, is below £300,000 then you may be able to use the annual accounting scheme.

Under this scheme you make 9 monthly direct debit payments based upon an estimate of the amount of VAT due. You must then prepare a VAT return for the year and send it in with the tenth balancing payment, by two months after the year end.

A different system is also available if the annual turnover is less than £100,000 and the net liability for VAT is less than £2,000 per annum. Under this scheme you will not be required to make any interim payments. If your net liability exceeds £2,000 per annum then you will only be required to make quarterly interim payments. The annual VAT return and balancing payment are again due within two months of the year end.

# PRACTICE EXAM BASED ASSESSMENT 1 UNIT 6

## SPORTS LTD

ANSWERS

# SECTION 1

## Task 1.1

**STOCK CARD**

**Product:** **Leather**

| | *Receipts* | | | *Issues* | | | *Balance* | |
|---|---|---|---|---|---|---|---|---|
| *Date* | *Quantity (metres)* | *Cost (per metre) £* | *Total Cost £* | *Quantity (metres)* | *Cost (per metre) £* | *Total Cost £* | *Quantity (metres)* | *Total Cost £* |
| B/f at 1 Nov | | | | | | | 10,000 | 10,000 |
| 5 Nov | 15,000 | 1.20 | 18,000 | | | | 25,000 | 28,000 |
| 12 Nov | | | | 10,000 | 1.00 | 10,000 | 15,000 | 18,000 |
| 19 Nov | 10,000 | 1.10 | 11,000 | | | | 25,000 | 29,000 |
| 26 Nov | | | | 20,000 | 1.20<br>1.10 | 18,000<br>5,500 | 5,000 | 5,500 |

## Task 1.2

| *Date* | *Code* | *Dr* | *Cr* |
|---|---|---|---|
| 5 November | 1000 | £18,000 | |
| 5 November | 3000 | | £18,000 |
| 12 November | 1100 | £10,000 | |
| 12 November | 1000 | | £10,000 |
| 19 November | 1000 | £11,000 | |
| 19 November | 3000 | | £11,000 |
| 26 November | 1100 | £23,500 | |
| 26 November | 1000 | | £23,500 |

## Task 1.3

Total cost of direct labour for November = £48,900.

| | | £ |
|---|---|---|
| 8,800 × £5 | = | 44,400 |
| 700 × £7 | = | 4,900 |
| | | 48,900 |

## Task 1.4

| *Fixed overheads for November* | *Basis* | *Total* £ | *Cutting* £ | *Finishing* £ | *Maintenance* £ |
|---|---|---|---|---|---|
| Machine insurance | NBV: 20:25:5 | 6,000 | 2,400 | 3,000 | 600 |
| Rent and other property overheads | Floor space 6:3:1 | 17,100 | 10,260 | 5,130 | 1,710 |
| Power costs | Allocated | 1,800 | 600 | 1,050 | 150 |
| Staff costs | Allocated | 20,250 | 5,940 | 4,770 | 9,540 |
| | | 45,150 | 19,200 | 13,950 | 12,000 |
| Maintenance | Time spent 40:60 | | 4,800 | 7,200 | (12,000) |
| | | 45,150 | 24,000 | 21,150 | - |

## Task 1.5

(a) The cutting department budgeted fixed overhead absorption rate for November = £2.50 per direct labour hour (£24,000/9,600h)

(b) The finishing department budgeted fixed overhead absorption rate for November = £3 per machine hour (£21,150/7,050h)

## Task 1.6

(a) (i) Production overhead absorbed for November in the cutting department = £23,125 (9,250 × £2.50)

(ii) Production overhead absorbed for November in the finishing department = £22,050 (7,350 × £3)

(b) (i) The cutting department overheads *underabsorbed* for November = £875 (£24,000 actual – £23,125 absorbed)

(ii) The finishing department production overheads *overabsorbed* for November = £900 (£22,050 absorbed – £21,150 actual)

(c) The cutting department production overhead underabsorbed will be debited in the profit and loss account, whilst the finishing department overheads overabsorbed will be credited to the profit and loss account for November.

# SECTION 2

## Task 2.1

| *Product* | *Exe* £ | *Wye* £ | *Zed* £ | *Total* £ |
|---|---|---|---|---|
| Sales revenue | 60,000 | 75,000 | 100,000 | 235,000 |
| Less: Variable costs | | | | |
| Direct materials | 20,000 | 24,000 | 30,000 | 74,000 |
| Direct labour | 5,000 | 6,000 | 10,000 | 21,000 |
| Total contribution | 35,000 | 45,000 | 60,000 | 140,000 |
| Fixed overheads | | | | 32,000 |
| Forecast profit | | | | 108,000 |

## Task 2.2

(a)

| *Product: Exe* | *Production volume* | |
|---|---|---|
| | *1,600 units* | *2,000 units* |
| Monthly variable costs | £20,000 | £25,000 |
| Monthly fixed costs | £32,000 | £32,000 |
| Total cost of production | £52,000 | £57,000 |
| Unit cost of production | £32.50 | £28.50 |

(b) The number of units of product Exe that the company would need to make and sell each month to make a profit of £2,000 is calculated below

Contribution – Fixed costs = Profits
Contribution – £32,000 = £2,000
Contribution = £34,000
(Contribution per unit × Quantity) = £34,000

$$\text{Quantity} = \frac{£34,000}{£17.50}$$

= 1,943 units

## Task 2.3

(a)

| *Product* | *Exe* | *Wye* | *Zed* |
|---|---|---|---|
| Unit contribution | £17.50 | £15.00 | £12.00 |
| Labour hours per unit | 0.5 | 0.4 | 0.4 |
| Contribution per labour hour | £35 | £37.50 | £30 |

(b) 2,000 Exe, 3,000 Wye and 2,000 Zed should be made and sold each month to maximise the company's profits using 3,000 labour hours.

| | |
|---|---|
| Total labour hours available | 3,000 |
| Less: used to make 3,000 Wye | (1,200) |
| | 1,800 |
| Less: used to make 2,000 Exe | (1,000) |
| Available labour hours to make Zed | 800 |

800 labour hours will be used to make 2,000 (800/0.4) Zed

## Task 2.4

(a) the payback period is 2 years and 11 months if the cash flows are assumed to occur evenly throughout the year or 3 years if they are assumed to occur at the year end.

| | | |
|---|---|---|
| | | £000 |
| Capital outlay at the start of the project | | (500) |
| Net inflows: | Year 1 | 60 |
| | | (440) |
| | Year 2 | 150 |
| | | (290) |
| | Year 3 | 320 |
| | | 30 |

Payback period = 2 years and 11 months $\left(\frac{290}{320}\times 12\right)$.

(b) The net present value is –£26,600

| | *Year 0* | *Year 1* | *Year 2* | *Year 3* | *Year 4* |
|---|---|---|---|---|---|
| | £000 | £000 | £000 | £000 | £000 |
| Net cashflows | (500) | 60 | 150 | 320 | 80 |
| Present value factors | 1.000 | 0.909 | 0.826 | 0.751 | 0.683 |
| Present values | (500) | 54.54 | 123.90 | 240.32 | 54.64 |
| Net present value | (26.60) | | | | |

**Task 2.5**

## MEMO

| | | | |
|---|---|---|---|
| **To:** | Managing Director | **Subject:** | Sports clothing project appraisal |
| **From:** | Accounting Technician | **Date:** | 12 December 2003 |

**The viability of the project**

The net present value (NPV) of the project is negative £26,600. This means that, when the time value of money is taken into consideration, the company would be worse off for undertaking the project. Therefore, on the basis of NPV alone and the information provided, I recommend that this project is rejected.

**Other information relevant to appraising the project**

1 The impact of sales of the new sports clothing on the existing products – footballs, and the proposed sports footwear – would need to be researched; the value of our brand might be strengthened by offering a larger range of products, so overall sales might increase; or if there is a limited market, sales might fall as customers divert their spending to the new product. Market research would be needed to establish this.

2 In addition, there is no information on whether cash inflows continue after year four, or whether the capital equipment purchased at the start of the project could be sold at the project's end. Further cash inflows of this nature could affect the decision regarding investment in this project.

Please contact me again if I can be of any further help to you in this matter.

# PRACTICE EXAM BASED ASSESSMENT 2 UNIT 6

# PLUMP LTD

ANSWERS

# SECTION 1

## Task 1.1

| STOCK CARD | | | | | | | | | |
|---|---|---|---|---|---|---|---|---|---|
| **Product:** | **Black cloth** | | | | | | | | |
| | *Receipts* | | | *Issues* | | | *Balance* | | |
| *Date* | *Quantity (metres)* | *Cost per metre £* | *Total cost* | *Quantity (metres)* | *Cost per metre £* | *Total cost* | *Quantity (metres)* | *Cost per metre* | *Total cost* |
| B/f at 1 May | | | | | | | 12,000 | 5.00 | 60,000 |
| 4 May | 10,000 | 5.44 | 54,400 | | | | 22,000 | 5.20 | 114,400 |
| 6 May | | | | 13,500 | 5.20 | 70,200 | 8,500 | 5.20 | 44,200 |
| 16 May | 15,000 | 5.36 | 80,400 | | | | 23,500 | 5.30 | 124,600 |
| 21 May | | | | 18,200 | 5.30 | 96,460 | 5,300 | 5.30 | 28,140 |
| 30 May | 20,000 | 4.90 | 98,000 | | | | 25,300 | 4.99 | 126,140 |

### WORKING

| | | Quantity (metres) | Cost per metre | Value £ |
|---|---|---|---|---|
| 1 May | opening balance | 12,000 | £5 | 60,000 |
| 4 May | purchase | 10,000 | £5.44 | 54,400 |
| Balance | | 22,000 | £114,400/22,000 = £5.20 | 114,400 |
| 6 May | issue | 13,500 | £5.20 | (70,200) |
| Balance | | 8,500 | | 44,200 |
| 16 May | purchase | 15,000 | £5.36 | 80,400 |
| Balance | | 23,500 | £124,600/23,500 = £5.30 | 124,600 |
| 21 May | issue | 18,200 | £5.30 | (96,460) |
| Balance | | 5,300 | | 28,140 |
| 30 May | purchase | 20,000 | £4.90 | 98,000 |
| Balance | | 25,300 | £126,140/25,300 = £4.99 | 126,140 |

## Task 1.2

| *Date* | *Code* | *Dr*<br>£ | *Cr*<br>£ |
|---|---|---|---|
| 4 May | 1030 | 54,400 | |
| | 4000 | | 54,400 |
| 6 May | 1200 | 70,200 | |
| | 1030 | | 70,200 |

## Task 1.3

**Wages control account**

| **Date** | **Account code** | **Description** | **£** | **Date** | **Account code** | **Description** | **£** |
|---|---|---|---|---|---|---|---|
| 31 May | 6000 | Cash at bank | 115,500 | 31 May | 1200 | Work in progress | 120,000 |
| 31 May | 4500 | Inland Revenue | 47,500 | 31 May | 1180 | Production overheads | 43,000 |
| | | | 163,000 | | | | 163,000 |

## Task 1.4

| *Overhead* | *Basis* | *Total* £ | *Warehouse* £ | *Manufacturing* £ | *Sales* £ | *Accounting* £ |
|---|---|---|---|---|---|---|
| Depreciation | Net book value | 10,000 | 1,000 | 8,000 | 400 | 600 |
| Rent | Floor space | 35,000 | 7,000 | 19,250 | 5,250 | 3,500 |
| Other property overheads | Floor space | 12,500 | 2,500 | 6,875 | 1,875 | 1,250 |
| Staff costs | Allocated | 39,650 | 2,800 | 6,925 | 15,875 | 14,050 |
| Other accounting overheads | Allocated | 13,600 | | | | 13,600 |
| | | 110,750 | 13,300 | 41,050 | 23,400 | 33,000 |
| Accounting | Apportioned | | 1,650 | 21,450 | 9,900 | (33,000) |
| | | 110,750 | 14,950 | 62,500 | 33,300 | - |

## Task 1.5

The budgeted fixed overhead absorption rate = £62,500/25,000 hours – £2.50 per hour

## Task 1.6

| **Manufacturing department** | *Budgeted activity (labour hours)* | | |
|---|---|---|---|
| | *25,000* | *30,000* | *32,500* |
| *Budgeted overheads* | May £ | £ | £ |
| Depreciation | 8,000 | 9,000 (W) | 9,000 |
| Rent | 19,250 | 19,250 | 19,250 |
| Other property overheads | 6,875 | 6,875 | 6,875 |
| Staff costs | 6,925 | 6,925 | 6,925 |
| Accounting | 21,450 | 21,450 | 21,450 |
| Total | 62,500 | 63,500 | 63,500 |
| Budgeted overhead absorption rate (rounded to nearest penny) | 2.50 | 2.12 | 1.95 |

**WORKING**

Increase in activity above 25,000 labour hours requires additional machinery costing £120,000 with a 10 year life, ie a depreciation charge of £12,000 per year or £1,000 per month. This machinery is related to the manufacturing process, so the entire additional depreciation of £1,000 is allocated to the manufacturing department.

## Task 1.7

| | *Budgeted overhead cost* |
|---|---|
| **Activity level** | **£** |
| 25,000 labour hours | 2 hours × £2.50 = £5.00 |
| 30,000 labour hours | 2 hours × £2.12 = £4.24 |
| 32,500 labour hours | 2 hours × £1.95 = £3.90 |

# SECTION 2

## Task 2.1

| | *Cost per batch* £ | *Cost per unit* £ |
|---|---|---|
| Direct materials – silk | 1,400 | 1.40 |
| – packaging | 120 | 0.12 |
| Direct labour | 600 | 0.60 |
| Cutting machine running costs | 80 | 0.08 |
| Other variable overheads | 180 | 0.18 |
| Total variable costs | 2,380 | 2.38 |
| Fixed overheads | 450 | 0.45 |
| Total cost | 2,830 | 2.83 |

## Task 2.2

(a) Contribution per unit = £5.50 – £2.38 = £3.12

(b) P/V ratio = 56.7%

$$\frac{\text{Contribution per unit}}{\text{Selling price per unit}} \times 100\% = \frac{£3.12}{£5.50} \times 100\%$$

(c) Budgeted fixed costs = £9,000

(20,000 x £0.45, **or** £7.50 per hour x 60 hours per batch x 20 batches)

(d) Breakeven quantity = 2,885 ties per annum

$$\frac{\text{Fixed costs}}{\text{Contribution per unit}} = \frac{£9,000}{£3.12}$$

In theory, 2,885 ties would need to be sold to break even. However, as the ties are manufactured in batches, the costs of a complete batch would be incurred for each production run. Therefore, more ties would need to be sold in order to cover the complete cost of the final batch. The answer above is consequently not strictly valid.

(e)

| | £ |
|---|---|
| Sales revenue (20,000 units) | 110,000 |
| Less: variable costs | 47,600 |
| Total contribution | 62,400 |
| Fixed overheads | 9,000 |
| Forecast profit | 53,400 |

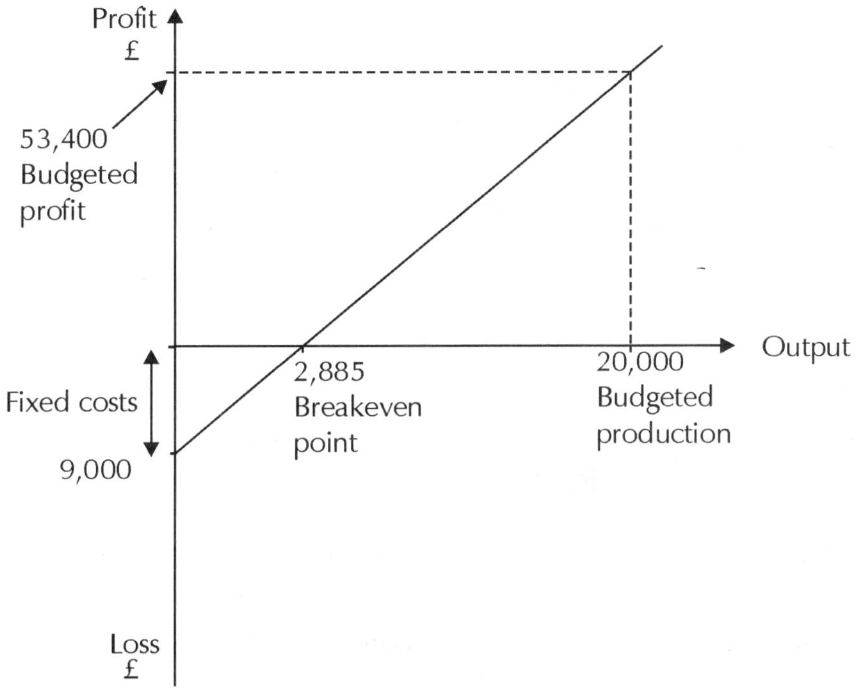


## Task 2.3

(a) The number of ties that need to be sold to make a profit of £70,000 = 25,321

| | |
|---|---|
| Contribution – fixed costs | = Profit |
| Contribution | = fixed costs + profit |
| | = £9,000 + £70,000 = £79,000 |
| Contribution per tie x number of ties sold | = £79,000 |
| £3.12 x number of ties sold | = £79,000 |
| Number of ties sold | =£79,000 / £3.12 |
| | = 25,321 |

(b) If the maximum number of labour hours available is 900 hours, the profit that would be made is £37,800

900 labour hours represents 900/60 = 15 batches
Profit from 15 batches is

| | £ |
|---|---|
| Contribution (15,000 x £3.12) | 46,800 |
| Less: fixed costs | 9,000 |
| | 37,800 |

**Task 2.4**

| | *Casual* | *Luxury* |
|---|---|---|
| Contribution per unit | £16 | £24 |
| Labour hours per unit | 1.5 | 2.5 |
| Contribution per labour hour | £10.67 | £9.60 |

**Task 2.5**

## REPORT

**To:** Managing Director

**Subject:** Production Mix: Casual and Luxury trousers

**From:** Accounting Technician

**Date:** 17 June 2003

**Unlimited capacity**

In this situation, as both lines of trousers give a positive contribution per unit, we will maximise profits by producing both lines to fulfil the maximum demand. Our production plan will be 500 pairs of Casual trousers and 300 pairs of Luxury trousers. The resulting profit from the venture is expected to be £6,200 (working 1).

**Limited labour hours**

With this constraint on production, we will maximise our profits by producing the line that yields the highest contribution per unit of the limiting factor; in other words, we should produce as many Casual trousers as are demanded, and utilise the remaining labour hours making Luxury trousers. The actual numbers are 500 pairs of Casual trousers and 60 pairs of Luxury trousers (working 2). The expected profit in this situation is £440 (working 3).

**WORKINGS**

1

| | £ |
|---|---|
| Contribution from casual trousers (500 x £16) | 8,000 |
| Contribution from luxury trousers (300 x £24) | 7,200 |
| Total contribution | 15,200 |
| Less: fixed costs | 9,000 |
| Profit | 6,200 |

2

| | | |
|---|---|---|
| Hours of labour time available | 900 | |
| Hours used making 500 pairs of casual trousers | 750 | (500 x 1.5) |
| Remaining hours | 150 | |

This means that 60 (150/2.5) pairs of Luxury trousers can be made.

3

| | £ |
|---|---|
| Contribution from casual trousers (500 x £16) | 8,000 |
| Contribution from luxury trousers (60 x £24) | 1,440 |
| Total contribution | 9,440 |
| Less: fixed costs | 9,000 |
| Profit | 440 |

# PRACTICE EXAM BASED ASSESSMENT 3 UNIT 6

# EASTLEY LTD

ANSWERS

# SECTION 1

## Task 1.1

| STOCK CARD | | | | | | |
|---|---|---|---|---|---|---|
| **Product:** | **Sugar** | | | | | |
| | *Receipts* | | | *Issues* | *Balance* | |
| *Date* | *Quantity (kgs)* | *Cost (per kg)* £ | *Total Cost* £ | *Quantity (kgs)* | *Quantity (kgs)* | *Total Cost* £ |
| B/f at 1 Nov | 50,000 | 1.00 | 50,000 | | 50,000 | 50,000 |
| 4 Nov | 20,000 | 1.20 | 24,000 | | 70,000 | 74,000 |
| 7 Nov | | | | 15,000 | 55,000 | 56,000 |
| 16 Nov | 35,000 | 0.90 | 31,500 | | 90,000 | 87,500 |
| 19 Nov | | | | 20,000 | 70,000 | 69,500 |
| 24 Nov | | | | 25,000 | 45,000 | 45,000 (w) |

**WORKING**

| | | £ |
|---|---|---|
| 24 Nov issue | 15,000kg @ 0.90 | 13,500 |
| | 5,000kg @ 1.20 | 6,000 |
| | 5,000kg @ 1.00 | 5,000 |
| | | 24,500 |

## Task 1.2

Use opening stock first:

| | kg |
|---|---|
| Opening stock | 50,000 |
| 7 Nov issue | (15,000) |
| | 35,000 |
| 19 Nov issue | (20,000) |
| | 15,000 |
| 24 Nov issue | (15,000) |
| | – |

| | | |
|---|---|---|
| 24 Nov issue – remainder | | 10,000kg @ £1.20 |
| | | £ |
| Remaining stock | 10,000 @ £1.20 | 12,000 |
| | 35,000 @ 0.90 | 31,500 |
| | | 43,500 |

## Task 1.3

| *OVERHEAD ALLOCATION AND APPORTIONMENT* | | | | | | |
|---|---|---|---|---|---|---|
| Budgeted fixed overheads for December 2002 | *Basis* | *Total* £ | *Manufacturing* £ | *Packing* £ | *Stores* £ | *Maintenance* £ |
| Depreciation | NBV | 4,800 | 4,320 | 192 | 96 | 192 |
| Rent | Floor space | 20,000 | 15,000 | 2,000 | 2,000 | 1,000 |
| Other property overheads | Floor space | 8,000 | 6,000 | 800 | 800 | 400 |
| Maintenance costs | Allocated | 15,200 | | | | 15,200 |
| Staff costs | Allocated | 19,400 | 4,650 | 1,800 | 8,750 | 4,200 |
| Total fixed overheads | | 67,400 | 29,970 | 4,792 | 11,646 | 20,922 |
| **Reapportionment:** | | | | | | |
| Maintenance | % of hours | | 14,695 | 4,198 | 2,099 | (20,922) |
| | | | | | 13,745 | |
| Stores | Requisitions | | 8,247 | 14,488 | (13,745) | |
| | | 67,400 | 52,912 | 14,488 | - | - |

## Task 1.4

Manufacturing $= \dfrac{£52{,}912}{2{,}100 \text{ hours}}$ = £25.20 per machine hour

Packing $= \dfrac{£14{,}488}{1{,}200 \text{ hours}}$ = £12.07 per direct labour hour

## Task 1.5

| | | | £ |
|---|---|---|---|
| Jasmine Pearl – | manufacturing | 3 hours × £25.20 = | 75.60 |
| | packing | 1 hour × £12.07 = | 12.07 |
| | | | 87.67 |
| King Pin – | manufacturing | 4.5 hours × £25.20 = | 113.40 |
| | packing | 1.5 hours × £12.07 = | 18.11 |
| | | | 131.51 |
| Lolly Desert – | manufacturing | 2.5 hours × £25.20 = | 63.00 |
| | | 2 hours × £12.07 = | 24.14 |
| | | | 87.14 |

## Task 1.6

# REPORT

**To:** Production manager

**From:** Accounting Technician

**Subject:** Absorption costing

**Date:** 2 December 2004

---

Total absorption costing is a method of costing products whereby all of the costs incurred in production both directly and indirectly are included in the product cost. This means in particular that the fixed production costs are allocated firstly to the production cost centres and are then absorbed into the cost of the product using the overhead absorption rate.

One of the main benefits of absorption costing is that it directs attention to the full cost of the product thereby the fixed production costs are not overlooked.

**Marginal costing**

An alternative method of costing products is to use marginal costing. Under this costing method the products are costed at their variable or marginal cost only. The fixed costs for the period are deducted in full from the profit and loss account. Marginal costing is useful for decision making purposes as the marginal cost will remain the same at different levels of production whereas the total absorption cost will alter at different levels of production as the fixed costs are spread over greater or fewer units.

**Marginal v absorption costing**

For costing purposes it can be argued that total absorption cost gives an indication of all the costs that have to be covered by income from the sale of the product. However for decision making purposes marginal costing is usually more useful.

There is one particular problem with absorption costing for reporting purposes in that it can potentially distort the profit shown from one period to another. Under absorption costing some of the fixed overheads of the business are included in the closing stock valuation which is carried forward to the charged to be next accounting period. If stock levels are changing then the profit will be distorted as either more or less fixed overhead is brought forward in opening stock and carried forward in closing stock.

## Task 1.7

| *Product: Pure Delight* | *Production* | |
|---|---|---|
| Production volume | 100,000 litres<br>£ | 125,000 litres<br>£ |
| Fixed costs | 12,500 | 12,500 |
| Variable costs | 60,000 | 75,000 |
| Total costs | 72,500 | 87,500 |
| Cost per 1,000 litres | £725 | £700 |

# SECTION 2

## Task 2.1

| | Production and sales level 320,000 litres £ |
|---|---|
| Sales (320,000 x £1.80) | 576,000 |
| Manufacturing costs (320,000 × £0.70) | 224,000 |
| Packing costs (320,000 × £0.30) | 96,000 |
| Property costs | 110,000 |
| Maintenance costs (£30,000 + (320,000 × 0.18)) | 87,600 |
| | 517,600 |
| Profit | £58,400 |

WORKINGS

Sales income per litre $= \dfrac{£540{,}000}{300{,}000 \text{ litres}} = £1.80$

OR $= \dfrac{£720{,}000}{400{,}000 \text{ litres}} = £1.80$

Manufacturing costs (variable) $= \dfrac{£210{,}000}{300{,}000 \text{ litres}} = £0.70$

As a check £280,000/400,000

Packing costs (variable) $= \dfrac{£90{,}000}{300{,}000 \text{ litres}} = £0.30$

As a check £120,000/400,000 = £0.30

**Property costs - fixed**

Maintenance costs – semi-variable

| Production | £ |
|---|---|
| 300,000 | 84,000 |
| 400,000 | 102,000 |
| 100,000 | 18,000 |

$$\text{Variable element} = \frac{£18,000}{10,000 \text{ litres}} = £0.18$$

| | £ |
|---|---|
| At 300,000 litres – total cost | 84,000 |
| Variable cost 300,000 × 0.18 | (54,000) |
| Fixed cost | 30,000 |

## Task 2.2

a) the breakeven sales in litres

**Variable cost per litre**

| | £ |
|---|---|
| Manufacturing cost | 0.70 |
| Packing cost | 0.30 |
| Maintenance | 0.18 |
| | 1.18 |

Contribution per litre = £1.80 – £1.18

= £0.62

**Fixed costs**

| | £ |
|---|---|
| Property | 110,000 |
| Maintenance | 30,000 |
| | 140,000 |

$$\text{Breakeven sales} = \frac{£140,000}{£0.62}$$

= 225,806 litres

(b) $$\text{Margin of safety} = \frac{320,000 - 225,806}{320,000} \times 100$$

= 29.4%

c) Level of sales to produce weekly profit of £100,000

$$= \frac{£140,000 + £100,000}{0.62} = 387,097 \text{ litres}$$

## Task 2.3

| | £ |
|---|---|
| Sales (360,000 × 1.80) | 648,000 |
| Manufacturing costs (360,000 × 0.70 × 90%) | 226,800 |
| Packing costs (360,000 × 0.30) | 108,000 |
| Property costs | 110,000 |
| Maintenance costs (360,000 × 0.18 + 30,000) | 94,800 |
| | 539,600 |
| Profit | £108,400 |

## Task 2.4

a) **Payback period if cash flows are assumed to take place at year end:**

| | Cash flow | Cumulative |
|---|---|---|
| | £ | £ |
| Year 1 | 180,000 | 180,000 |
| Year 2 | 150,000 | 330,000 |
| Year 3 | 120,000 | 450,000 |
| Year 4 | 100,000 | 550,000 |

Payback period = 4 years

**Payback period if cash flows are assumed to occur evenly throughout year:**

Payback period = 3 years + 50,000/100,000

= 3.5 years

b) **Net present value**

| Year | Cash flow | Discount factor | Present value |
|---|---|---|---|
| | £ | | £ |
| 0 | (500,000) | 1.000 | (500,000) |
| 1 | 180,000 | 0.926 | 166,680 |
| 2 | 150,000 | 0.857 | 128,550 |
| 3 | 120,000 | 0.794 | 95,280 |
| 4 | 100,000 | 0.735 | 73,500 |
| 5 | 80,000 | 0.681 | 54,480 |
| Net present value | | | 18,490 |

c)

# MEMO

**To:** Finance Director

**From:** Accounting Technician

**Subject:** Machinery Investment

**Date:** 2 December 2004

---

The Production Manager has provided me with some figures regarding the purchase of new machinery and the cost savings that could be made with this machinery.

I have calculated that the payback period for the investment would be 4 years if it was assumed that the savings were made at the end of each year and 3.5 years if it was assumed that the cash flows occurred evenly throughout the year.

I have also calculated the net present value of the project using the company's cost of capital of 8%. The investment has a positive net present value of £18,490. In the net present value calculations it was assumed that the machine would be purchased immediately and that the cost savings would occur at the end of each year.

The positive net present value indicates the proposed investment is financially worthwhile.

## Task 2.5

A net present value is the net total of all of the cash flows of a project after those cash flows have been discounted to take account of the time value of money. A positive net present value means that even after taking account of the time value of money the business will be better off if it invests in the project.

## Task 2.6

The internal rate of return of a project is the discount which gives a net present value of zero.

# PRACTICE EXAM BASED ASSESSMENT 4 UNIT 6

# GIFT LTD (AAT SPECIMEN)

ANSWERS

# SECTION 1

## Task 1.1

| STOCK CARD | | | | | | | | |
|---|---|---|---|---|---|---|---|---|
| **Product:** | **Pink plastic** | | | | | | | |
| | *Receipts* | | | *Issues* | | | *Balance* | |
| *Date* | *Quantity kgs* | *Cost per kg* £ | *Total Cost* £ | *Quantity kgs* | *Cost per kg* £ | *Total Cost* £ | *Quantity kgs* | *Total Cost* £ |
| B/f at 1.11.03 | | | | | | | 10,000 | 10,000 |
| 6.11.03 | 20,000 | 1.10 | 22,000 | | | | 30,000 | 32,000 |
| 11.11.03 | | | | 16,000 | 10,000 × 1.00<br>6,000 × 1.10 | 10,000<br>6,000<br>16,600 | 14,000 | 15,400 |
| 17.11.03 | 10,000 | 1.20 | 12,000 | | | | 24,000 | 27,400 |
| 19.11.03 | | | | 20,000 | 14,000 × 1.10<br>6,000 × 1.20 | 16,400<br>7,200<br>22,800 | 4,000 | 4,800 |

## Task 1.2

| Date | Code | Dr | Cr |
|---|---|---|---|
| 6 Nov | 1000 | 22,000 | |
| 6 Nov | 3000 | | 22,000 |
| 11 Nov | 1000 | | 16,600 |
| 11 Nov | 1100 | 16,600 | |
| 17 Nov | 1000 | 12,000 | |
| 17 Nov | 3000 | | 12,000 |
| 19 Nov | 1000 | | 22,600 |
| 19 Nov | 1100 | 22,600 | |

## Task 1.3

| | | |
|---|---|---|
| Normal rate | 12,000 hours x £6 | £72,000 |
| Overtime premium | 1,400 hours x £3 | £4,200 |
| Total direct labour cost | | £76,200 |

## Task 1.4

| *Fixed overheads for November* | *Basis* | *Total* £ | *Warehouse* £ | *Manufacturing* £ | *Sales* £ | *Accounting* £ |
|---|---|---|---|---|---|---|
| Depreciation | Net book value | 7,400 | 1,665 | 4,995 | | 740 |
| Rent | Floor space | 2,500 | 375 | 1,750 | 250 | 125 |
| Other property overheads | Floor space | 3,200 | 480 | 2,240 | 320 | 160 |
| Accounting overheads | Allocated | 6,250 | | | | 6,250 |
| Staff costs | Allocated | 18,825 | 4,230 | 3,015 | 6,520 | 5,160 |
| | | 38,275 | 6,750 | 12,000 | 7,090 | 12,435 |

## Task 1.5

Budgeted fixed overhead aborption rate = £12,000/20,000 = £0.60

## Task 1.6

| Product: Meg Doll | £ |
|---|---|
| **Direct costs** | |
| Pink plastic | 39,200 |
| Direct labour | 76,200 |
| **Indirect costs** | |
| Manufacturing department overheads | 7,200 |
| Total cost of production | 122,600 |
| Number of Meg dolls produced | 36,000 |
| Unit cost of production (to the nearest penny) | 3.41 |

# SECTION 2

## Task 2.1

| Product | E<br>£ | C<br>£ | R<br>£ |
|---|---|---|---|
| Selling price per unit | 30.00 | 40.00 | 60.00 |
| Less: Unit variable costs | | | |
| Direct materials | 10.00 | 11.00 | 12.00 |
| Direct labour | 16.00 | 16.00 | 20.00 |
| Variable overheads | 2.00 | 1.75 | 7.00 |
| Contribution per unit | 2.00 | 11.25 | 21.00 |

## Task 2.2

Number of units = £4,800/£2 = 2,400 units

## Task 2.3

| Product | E | C | R |
|---|---|---|---|
| Contribution per unit | £2.00 | £11.25 | £21.0 |
| Machine hours per unit | 0.1 | 0.15 | 0.35 |
| Contribution per machine hour | £20.00 | £75.00 | £60.00 |

## Task 2.4

The products should be ranked by contribution per limiting factor, in this case machine hours. The ranking is as follows:

1 **Product C**
2 **Product R**
3 **Product E**

Total available machine hours = 365 hours. Based on the ranking above:

Use **225 hours** to manufacture **1,500 units of C**
Use **140 hours** to manufacture **400 units of R**
**No units of E** should be manufactured.

## Task 2.5

a) The payback period required to recoup an investment of £80,000 from one year is as follows:

| | | | |
|---|---|---|---|
| From year two | £15,000 | Outstanding investment | £65,000 |
| From year three | £25,000 | Outstanding investment | £40,000 |

In year four, the product generates £80,000, so the extra time needed to pay back the investment is six months.

Total payback period is **two years and six months.**

b)

| | Year 1 | Year 2 | Year 3 | Year 4 | Year 5 |
|---|---|---|---|---|---|
| | £000 | £000 | £000 | £000 | £000 |
| Design costs | (80) | | | | |
| Sales revenues | | 30 | 50 | 160 | 50 |
| Variable costs | | (15) | (25) | (80) | (25) |
| Net cashflows | (80) | 15 | 25 | 80 | 25 |
| Present value factor | 0.909 | 0.826 | 0.751 | 0.683 | 0.621 |
| Present value | (72.7) | 12.4 | 18.8 | 54.6 | 15.5 |

**Net present value = £28,600**

## Task 2.6

# REPORT

To: Managing Director    From: Candidate    Date: Dec 03

The net present value technique relies on discounting relevant cashflows at an appropriate rate of return. It would be helpful to know:

1 Whether there are any additional cashflows beyond year five.

2 Whether the introduction of a new product will affect sales of the existing products E, C and R.

On the basis of the information provided, the project has a positive net present value of £28,600 and should be carried out.

# AAT

## SAMPLE SIMULATION
## UNIT 6

## QUALITY CANDLES LTD

ANSWERS

## Task 1

### STORES RECORD CARD

Materials description: Candlewick thread, 200 metre rolls
Code no: CW728

Maximum quantity: 400
Minimum quantity: 140
Reorder level: 230
Reorder Quantity: 80

| | Receipts | | | | Issues | | | | Stock balance | | |
|---|---|---|---|---|---|---|---|---|---|---|---|
| Date 2003 | Document number | Qty | Price per roll (£) | Total (£) | Document number | Qty | Price per Roll (£) | Total (£) | Qty | Price per roll (£) | Total (£) |
| 1 Oct | | | | | | | | | 28<br>26 | 2.20<br>2.30 | 61.60<br>59.80 |
| | | | | | | | | | 54 | | 121.40 |
| 3 Oct | | | | | 249 | 26<br>4 | 2.30<br>2.20 | 59.50<br>8.80 | | | |
| | | | | | | 30 | | 68.80 | 24 | 2.20 | 52.80 |
| 6 Oct | 419 | 80 | 235 | 188.00 | | | | | 24<br>80 | 2.20<br>2.35 | 52.80<br>188.00 |
| | | | | | | | | | 104 | | 240.80 |
| 8 Oct | | | | | 252 | 40 | 2.35 | 94.00 | 24<br>40 | 2.20<br>2.35 | 52.80<br>94.00 |
| | | | | | | | | | 64 | | 146.80 |
| 9 Oct | 427 | 80 | 2.38 | 190.40 | | | | | 24<br>40<br>80 | 2.20<br>2.35<br>2.38 | 52.80<br>94.00<br>190.40 |
| | | | | | | | | | 144 | | 337.20 |
| 10 Oct | 75 | 3 | 2.35 | 7.05 | | | | | 24<br>43<br>80 | 2.20<br>2.35<br>2.38 | 52.80<br>101.05<br>190.40 |
| | | | | | | | | | 147 | | 344.25 |

## Task 2

### MATERIALS REQUISITION

Department: Manufacturing

Document no: 252

Date: 08/10/2003

| Code no | Description | Quantity | **Cost office use only** Value of issue (£) |
| --- | --- | --- | --- |
| CW728 | Candlewick thread 200m rolls | 40 | 94.00 |

**Received by:** ............................................ **Signature:** ............................................

### MATERIALS RETURNED

Department: Manufacturing

Document no: 75

Date: 10/10/2003

| Code no | Description | Quantity | **Cost office use only** Value of issue(£) |
| --- | --- | --- | --- |
| CW728 | Candlewick thread 200m rolls | 3 | 7.05 |

**Received by:** ............................................ **Signature:** ............................................

## Task 3

# MEMO

**To:** General Manager
**From:** Bobby Forster, Accounts Assistant
**Subject:** Stock levels of candlewick thread, week ending 10 October 2003
**Date:** 14 October 2003

---

The stock levels on this item have been a cause for concern during the last week.

The stock level began the week below the minimum quantity of 140 rolls and, although two deliveries brought the balance to 147 rolls by the end of the week, it is clear that the minimum level is soon to be reached once more.

This could lead to the company running out of stock before a new batch of candlewick is received from the supplier. Customer orders could be lost or it may be necessary to pay high prices to acquire urgent supplies.

I suggest that we should review the stock control levels and reorder quantity. Perhaps usage patterns have changed since the levels were set. If this is the case the levels and the reorder quantity should be recalculated, taking account of any changes in usage patterns and supply lead times.

I would be happy to discuss the problem with you at any time.

## Task 4

**QUALITY CANDLES LIMITED**
**PIECEWORK OPERATION CARD**

Operative name Mary Roberts Department: Manufacturing

Clock number R27

Week beginning 6 October 2003

| Activity | Monday | Tuesday | Wednesday | Thursday | Friday |
|---|---|---|---|---|---|
| Batches produced | 120 | 102 | 34 | 202 | 115 |
| Batches rejected | 5 | 7 | 4 | 11 | 5 |
| Batches accepted | 115 | 95 | 30 | 191 | 110 |
| Rate per batch | £ 0.50 | £ 0.50 | £ 0.50 | £ 0.50 | £ 0.50 |
| Piecework payment | £ 57.50 | £ 47.50 | £ 15.00 | £ 95.50 | £ 55.00 |
| Bonus payable | £ 2.30 | £ nil | £ nil | £ nil | £ 2.20 |
| **Total payable for day*** | £ 59.80 | £ 50.00 | £ 50.00 | £ 95.50 | £ 57.20 |

**Total wages payable for week:**

| | £ |
|---|---|
| Direct wages | 308.00 |
| Indirect wages | 4.50 |
| Total wages | 312.50 |

* Guaranteed daily wage of £50 is payable if piecework payment plus bonus amounts less than £50

Supervisor's signature: *A Peters*

## Task 5

### INTERNAL MEMO

**To:** Roy Hart, Manufacturing Department Supervisor
**From:** Bobby Forster, Accounts Assistant
**Subject:** Discrepancy on piecework operation card
**Date:** 10 October 2003

---

I have a query on a piecework operation card for the week beginning 6 October, a copy of which is attached. The employee concerned is Mary Roberts, clock number R27.

The output recorded for Wednesday is exceptionally low and correspondingly the output for Thursday is very high. It is possible that some of the output for Wednesday was recorded in error for Thursday. This distorts the wages payable because of the guaranteed daily rate.

Could you please look into this for me, to see whether there was in fact a genuine reason for the unusual pattern in output levels.

Thank you for your help.

## Task 6

**Production overhead analysis sheet for 2004**

| Production overhead item | Total £000 | Manufacturing £000 | Painting/ finishing £000 | Packing £000 | Stores £000 | Maintenance £000 |
|---|---|---|---|---|---|---|
| Indirect labour | 98 | 22 | 14 | 11 | 35 | 16 |
| Indirect materials | 40 | 12 | 2 | 2 | 12 | 12 |
| Rent and rates | 105 | 45 | 15 | 24 | 12 | 9 |
| Protective clothing | 31 | 31 | | | | |
| Power | 40 | 20 | 4 | 12 | 2 | 2 |
| Insurance | 24 | 11 | 4 | 6 | 2 | 1 |
| Heat and Light | 35 | 15 | 5 | 8 | 4 | 3 |
| Depreciation | 48 | 22 | 8 | 12 | 4 | 2 |
| Other | 15 | 5 | 5 | 5 | | |
| **Total department overheads** | 436 | 183 | 57 | 80 | 71 | 45 |
| **Apportion maintenance total** | – | 21 | 12 | 9 | 3 | (45) |
| **Apportion stores total** | – | 36 | 20 | 18 | (74) | |
| **Total production dept overheads** | 436 | 240 | 89 | 107 | | |

## Task 7

**Working paper**

**Calculation of production overhead absorption rates for 2004**

*Manufacturing department*

Machine hour rate $= \dfrac{£240,000}{200,000}$

$= £1.20$ per machine hour

*Painting and finishing department*

Labour hour rate $= \dfrac{£89,000}{28,000}$

$= £3.18$ per labour hour

*Packing department*

Machine hour rate $= \dfrac{£107,000}{90,000}$

$= £1.19$ per machine hour

## Task 8

**Sample calculations: working paper**

**Reversing the order of service department re-apportionments**

| Production overhead item | Total £000 | Manufacturing £000 | Painting/ finishing £000 | Packing £000 | Stores £000 | Maintenance £000 |
|---|---|---|---|---|---|---|
| **Total department overheads (from task 6)** | 436 | 183 | 57 | 80 | 71 | 45 |
| **Apportion stores total** | – | 27 | 15 | 13 | (71) | 16 |
| **Apportion maintenance total** | – | 31 | 17 | 13 | – | (61) |
| **Total production dept overheads** | 436 | 241 | 89 | 106 | | |

**Task 9**

## INTERNAL MEMO

**To:** General Manager
**From:** Bobby Forster, Accounts Assistant
**Subject:** Re-apportionment of service department costs
**Date:** 5 November 2003

---

I have carried out the analysis you requested and the results are attached.

As you will see, the change in method does not result in a material difference in the total overhead for each production cost centre. Therefore I suggest that we should not change our apportionment methods since the value of the management information would not be materially affected by the change.

**Task 10**

**Journal entry for production overheads**

**October 2003**

*Entries for overhead absorbed during the month*

| | Debit (£) | Credit(£) |
|---|---|---|
| Work in progress: manufacturing dept | 18,500 | |
| Work in progress: painting and finishing dept | 7,400 | |
| Work in progress: packing dept | 8,300 | |
| Production overhead control | | 34,200 |

*Entries for overhead under/over absorbed during the month*

| | Debit (£) | Credit(£) |
|---|---|---|
| Overhead over/under absorbed (P+L) | | 18,400 |
| Production overhead control | 18,400 | |

## INTERNAL MEMO

**To:** Production Manager
**From:** Bobby Forster, Accounts Assistant
**Subject:** Overhead absorption for October 2003
**Date:** 9 November 2003

---

A significant over absorption arose during the month. The total amount over absorbed was £18,400 compared with total actual expenditure of £15,800.

Could you please check the data for me to ensure that no recording errors have occurred?

The actual production overhead figure may be too low, perhaps because of miscoding of invoices. Alternatively, the activity data for the production departments may have been recorded incorrectly.

Thank you for your help.

## Task 11

**Workings for determination of revenue and cost behaviour patterns**

*Sales revenue*

Selling price per case = £28,000/7,000 = £4

Check: 6,200 x £4 = £24,800; 5,900 x £4 = £23,600

*Candles cost*

Candle cost per case = £9,100/7,000 = £1.30

Check: 6,200 x £1.30 = £8,060; 5,900 x £1.30 = £7,670

*Packing materials cost*

Packing materials cost per case = £5,250/7,000 = £0.75

Check: 6,200 x £0.75 = £4,650; 5,900 x £0.75 = £4,425

*Packing labour cost*

Packing labour cost per case = £2,100/7,000 = £0.30

Check: 6,200 x £0.30 = £1,860; 5,900 x £0.30 = £1,770

*Packing overhead cost*

| | Cases | £ |
|---|---|---|
| High | 7,000 | 5,400 |
| Low | 5,900 | 5,180 |
| Difference | 1,100 | 220 |

Variable cost per case = £220/1,100 = £0.20. Fixed cost = £5,400 – (7,000 x £0.20) = £4,000

Check: for 6,200 cases cost is £4,000 + (6,200 x £0.20) = £5,240

*Other overhead cost*

Fixed cost = £2,500 per month

**Quality Candles Limited: mail order division**
**Planned results for December 2003**

| | December |
|---|---|
| Number of cases to be sold | 6,800 |
| | £ |
| Candles cost (@ £1.30) | 8,840 |
| Packing materials cost (@ £0.75) | 5,100 |
| Packing labour cost (@ £0.30) | 2,040 |
| Packing overhead cost | 5,360 |
| Other overhead cost | 2,500 |
| Total costs | 23,840 |
| Sales revenue (@ £4) | 27,200 |
| Profit | 3,360 |

**Space for workings**

*Packing overhead cost*

| | £ |
|---|---|
| Fixed | 4,000 |
| Variable (6,800 x £0.20) | 1,360 |
| | 5,360 |

## Task 12(i)

**Quality Candles Limited: mail order division**
**Planned results for December 2003: increased activity**

| | December |
|---|---|
| Number of cases to be sold | 7,600 |
| | £ |
| Candles cost (@ £1.30) | 9,880 |
| Packing materials cost (@ £0.60) | 4,560 |
| Packing labour cost (@ £0.30) | 2,280 |
| Packing overhead cost | 5,520 |
| Other overhead cost | 2,500 |
| Total costs | 24,740 |
| Sales revenue (@ £4) | 30,400 |
| Profit | 5,660 |

**Space for workings**

*Packing overhead cost*

| | £ |
|---|---|
| Fixed | 4,000 |
| Variable (7,600 x £0.20) | 1,520 |
| | 5,520 |

## Task 12(ii)

**Quality Candles Limited: mail order division**
**Planned results for December 2003: increased activity**

*Calculation of breakeven point and margin of safety: working paper*

| | £ | £ |
|---|---|---|
| Contribution per case: | | |
| Selling price | | 4.00 |
| Less variable costs: | | |
| Candles | 1.30 | |
| Packing materials | 0.60 | |
| Packing labour | 0.30 | |
| Packing overhead | 0.20 | |
| | | 2.40 |
| Contribution per case | | 1.60 |
| Fixed overhead: | | |
| Packing overhead | | 4,000 |
| Other overhead | | 2,500 |
| | | 6,500 |

*Breakeven point*

Number of cases to break even $= \frac{£6{,}500}{£1.60}$

= 4,063 cases

Margin of safety = 7,600 – 4,063 cases

= 3,537 cases

= 47% of planned activity

**Task 12(iii)**

## INTERNAL MEMO

**To:** General Manager
**From:** Bobby Forster, Accounts Assistant
**Subject:** Mail order division: bulk discounts for December 2003
**Date:** 11 November 2003

---

I have evaluated the proposal to increase sales and take advantage of a bulk discount for packing materials.

The planned profit will increase considerably to £5,660 for the month compared with £3,360 without the increased activity. The breakeven point will be 4,063 cases which results in a margin of safety of 47% of planned activity.

Since the company is looking for opportunities to increase profit, the high profit and the wide margin of safety mean that this represents a very attractive proposal.

However the following assumptions affect the validity of the projections.

- The increased sales volume can be achieved at the current selling price. It is possible that the selling price would have to be reduced in order to sell the greater output.
- All other unit variable costs and fixed costs will not be altered by the increase in activity. Since the volume projection is outside the range for which data is available this may not be a valid assumption. For example it may be necessary to pay overtime rates to labour in order to achieve the increased output.
- The increased volume can be achieved with the existing packing and delivery capacity.

Please let me know if you require any further information.

## Task 13(i)

**Working paper for the financial appraisal of purchase of delivery vehicles**

| Year | Cashflow £ | Discount factor @ 12% | Present value £ |
|---|---|---|---|
| 2003 | -90,000 | 1.000 | -90,000 |
| 2004 | 34,800 | 0.893 | 31,076 |
| 2005 | 34,800 | 0.797 | 27,736 |
| 2006 | 34,800 | 0.712 | 24,778 |
| 2007 | 39,800 | 0.636 | 25,313 |
| Net present value | | | 18,903 |

**Working space for calculation of payback period**

| | Cumulative cashflow (£) |
|---|---|
| 2003 | -90,000 |
| 2004 | -55,200 |
| 2005 | -20,400 |
| 2006 | 14,400 |

Payback period = 2 years + (20,400/34,800) = 2.6 years

## Task 13(ii)

### INTERNAL MEMO

**To:** General Manager
**From:** Bobby Forster, Accounts Assistant
**Subject:** Purchase of delivery vehicles for mail order division
**Date:** 14 November 2003

---

The proposal to purchase delivery vehicles is acceptable from a financial viewpoint because it returns a positive net present value of £18,903 at a discount rate of 12%. This calculation assumes that all cashflows occur at the end of each year.

The payback period is between two and three years. If we assume even cashflows during the year the payback period can be calculated as 2.6 years. This is acceptable since it is shorter than the company requirement of three years, although there is not much room for error in the cashflow calculations.

Please let me know if I can help any further with the evaluation.

# AAT SAMPLE SIMULATION
# UNIT 7

# HOMER LTD

ANSWERS

## Task 1

**Sales to external customers**
**Manufacturing and Sales divisions combined**

| | Monthly totals £'000 | Cumulative total for the year £'000 |
|---|---|---|
| **2001/2002** | | |
| April | 384 | 384 |
| May | 271 | 655 |
| June | 222 | 877 |
| July | 309 | 1,186 |
| August | 346 | 1,532 |
| September | 262 | 1,794 |
| October | 240 | 2,034 |
| November | 329 | 2,363 |
| December | 279 | 2,642 |
| January | 277 | 2,919 |
| February | 244 | 3,163 |
| March | 385 | 3,548 |
| **2002/2003** | | |
| April | 381 | 381 |
| May | 242 | 623 |
| June | 237 | 860 |
| July | 339 | 1,199 |
| August | 330 | 1,529 |
| September | 299 | 1,828 |
| October | 231 | 2,059 |
| November | 372 | 2,431 |
| December | 355 | 2,786 |
| January | 310 | 3,096 |
| February | 272 | 3,368 |
| March | 291 | 3,659 |

**Notes**

1. In the first column, enter the monthly total of external sales achieved by the two divisions.
2. In the second column, enter the cumulative total of external sales in the accounting year.

**Task 2**

**Cumulative external sales 2001/2002 and 2002/2003**

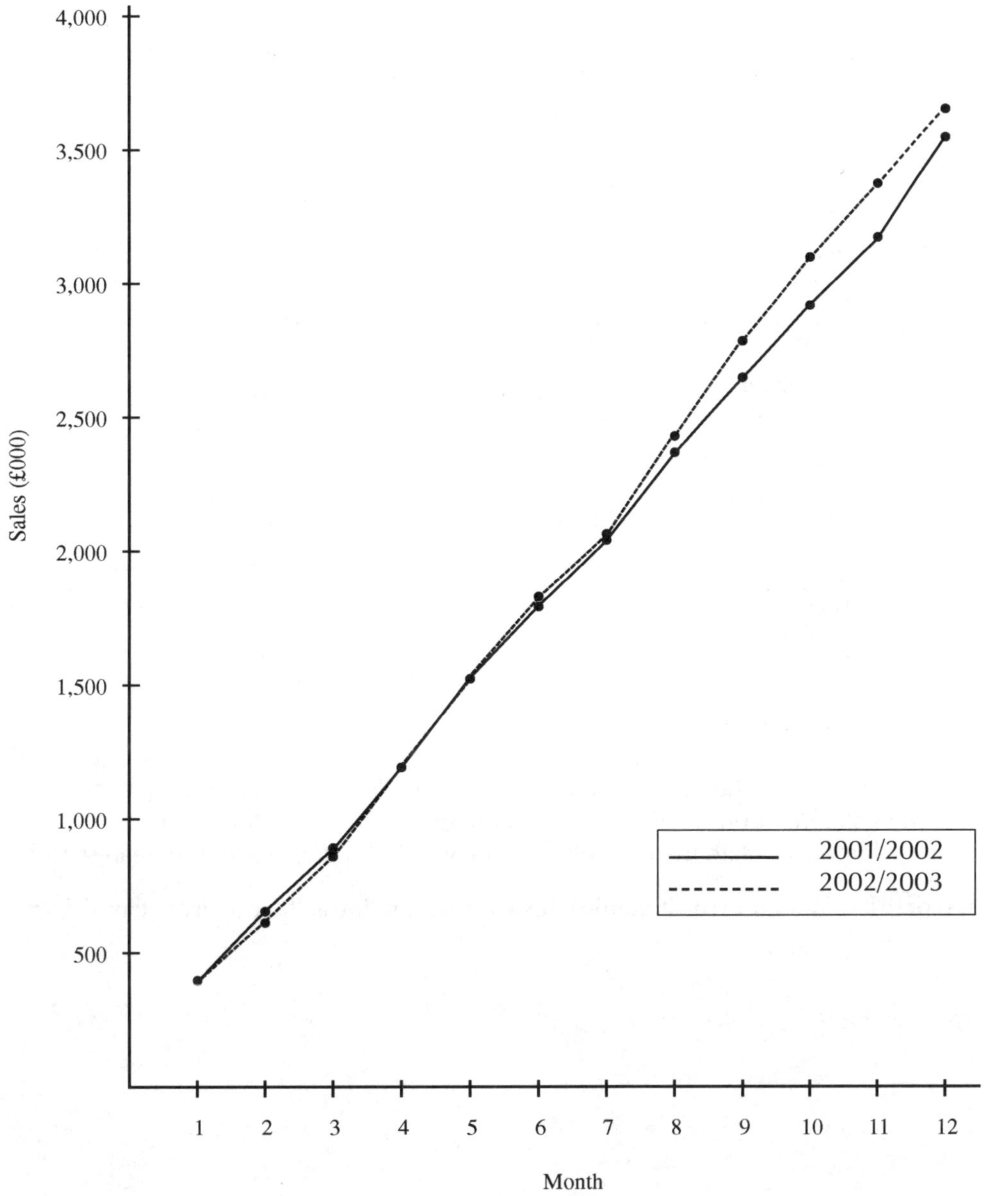

## Task 3

**Indexed sales to external customers**
**Manufacturing and Sales divisions combined**

| | Unadjusted totals £'000 | Index factor | Indexed totals £'000 |
|---|---|---|---|
| **2002/2003** | | | |
| April | 381 | 131.0/123.8 | 403 |
| May | 242 | 131.0/124.4 | 255 |
| June | 237 | 131.0/124.9 | 249 |
| July | 339 | 131.0/125.7 | 353 |
| August | 330 | 131.0/126.3 | 342 |
| September | 299 | 131.0/127.0 | 308 |
| October | 231 | 131.0/127.5 | 237 |
| November | 372 | 131.0/128.1 | 380 |
| December | 355 | 131.0/128.9 | 361 |
| January | 310 | 131.0/129.6 | 313 |
| February | 272 | 131.0/130.2 | 274 |
| March | 291 | 131.0/131.0 | 291 |

**Notes**

1. In the first column, insert the monthly totals of external sales calculated in Task 1.
2. In the second column, insert the index factor required to convert to March 2003 values.
3. In the third column, calculate the monthly sales in March 2003 terms (to the nearest £1,000).

**Note to assessors: it is not an error if candidates express the index factors in decimal form.**

**Task 4**

## LOAN APPLICATION (extract)

| | | |
|---|---|---|
| Name of applicant company | | Homer Limited |
| Latest year for which accounting information is available | | Year ended 31 March 2003 |
| *Total sales revenue* | | |
| In latest year for which accounts are available | £ | 3,659,000 |
| In previous year | £ | 3,548,000 |
| Percentage change (+/-) | | +3.13% |
| *Net profit after all expenses, before taxation* | | |
| In latest year for which accounts are available | £ | 310,000 |
| In previous year | £ | 278,000 |
| Percentage change (+/-) | | +11.51% |
| *Gross profit margin (%)* | | 40.17% |
| Net profit margin (%) | | 8.47% |
| Return on capital employed (%) | | 4.70% |

**Notes**

1. In the case of a company with a divisional structure, all figures should refer to the results of the company as a whole, not to individual divisions within the company.
2. Unless otherwise stated, all questions relate to the latest year for which accounting information is available.
3. Figures should be actual historical values, with no indexing for inflation.
4. Return on capital employed is defined as net profit for the year before taxation, divided by total capital employed.

## MEMO

**To:** Sonia Liesl
**From:** Amir Pindhi
**Subject:** Loan application form
**Date:** 14 April 2003

---

I attach the completed loan application form for your approval before its submission to the bank.

If it is in order, I assume you will forward the form to the bank for processing. However, if you need further clarification please come back to me.

## MEMO

**To:** Sonia Liesl
**From:** Amir Pindhi
**Subject:** Ratios and performance indicators for the year ended 31 March 2003
**Date:** 14 April 2003

---

Here are the required ratios and performance indicators for the year ended 31 March 2003.

Gross profit percentage: 40.17%. This has fallen from 43.15% in the previous year, possibly because of higher production costs (see 'production cost per unit' below).

Net profit percentage: 8.47%. Despite the fall in GPP, this has risen from 7.84% in the previous year, possibly because of tighter control of overheads.

Production cost per unit: (£2,190,000/199,000=) £11.01. This has risen from £10.83 in the previous year, possibly because of higher materials costs.

Value of sales earned per employee: (£3,659,000/143=) £25,587.41. This has fallen from £26,018.13, possibly because increases in sales have not kept step with increases in the number of employees.

**Task 6**

# Value Added Tax Return

**For the period**

01-01-03 **to** 31-03-03

HM Customs and Excise

**For Official Use**

| Registration number | Period |
|---|---|
| 625 7816 29 | 03 03 |

HOMER LIMITED
SESTOS DRIVE
PANTILE TRADING ESTATE
CV32 1AW

**You could be liable to a financial penalty if your completed return and all the VAT payable are not received by the due date.**

**Due date:** 30.04.03

**For official use D O R only**

Fold Here

**Before you fill in this form please read the notes on the back and the VAT leaflet *"Filling in your VAT return"*.** Fill in all boxes clearly in ink, and write 'none' where necessary. Don't put a dash or leave any box blank. If there are no pence write "00" in the pence column. **Do not** enter more than one amount in any box.

**For official use**

| | | £ | p |
|---|---|---|---|
| VAT due in this period on **sales** and other outputs | 1 | 139,618 | 95 |
| VAT due in this period on **acquisitions** from other **EC Member States** | 2 | NONE | |
| Total VAT due **(the sum of boxes 1 and 2)** | 3 | 139,618 | 95 |
| VAT reclaimed in this period on **purchases** and other inputs (including acquisitions from the EC) | 4 | 91,197 | 54 |
| Net VAT to be paid to Customs or reclaimed by you **(Difference between boxes 3 and 4)** | 5 | 48,421 | 41 |
| Total value of **sales** and all other outputs excluding any VAT. **Include your box 8 figure** | 6 | 873,012 | 00 |
| Total value of **purchases** and all other inputs excluding any VAT. **Include your box 9 figure** | 7 | 520,568 | 00 |
| Total value of all **supplies** of goods and related services, excluding any VAT, to other **EC Member States** | 8 | 75,190 | 00 |
| Total value of all **acquisitions** of goods and related services, excluding any VAT, from other **EC Member States** | 9 | NONE | 00 |

If you are enclosing a payment please tick this box. ✔

DECLARATION: You, or someone on your behalf, must sign below.

I, SONIA LIESL declare that the
(Full name of signatory in BLOCK LETTERS)

information given above is true and complete.

Signature ............................ Date ............................

**A false declaration can result in prosecution.**

**VAT 100** (Full) IB(October 2000)

## Task 7

# HOMER LIMITED

Sestos Drive, Pantile Trading Estate CV32 1AW
Telephone: 02467 881235

14 April 2003

H M Customs and Excise
Bell House
33 Lambert Road
Coventry
CV12 8TR

Dear Sir/Madam

This company is considering the idea of importing raw materials from a Far Eastern supplier. We are unsure of the VAT implications of doing this.

I would be grateful if you would send me a copy of any relevant publication dealing with VAT on imports.

Yours faithfully

Sonia Liesl
ACCOUNTANT

Registered office: Sestos Drive, Pantile Trading Estate CV32 1AW
Registered in England, number 2007814

## Task 8

# MEMO

**To:** Sonia Liesl
**From:** Amir Pindhi
**Subject:** VAT on imports
**Date:** 14 April 2003

I enclose a draft letter to the local VAT office requesting copies of publications on this topic.

Briefly, the rule is that if we import goods from a non-EC country we have to pay VAT on import at the standard rate. It will normally be possible to reclaim this as recoverable VAT.

It may be possible to arrange the imports through an appropriate agent (one who is approved for duty deferment). If so, we can then defer the payment.

# AAT

## PRACTICE SIMULATION
## UNIT 7

## HODDLE LTD

ANSWERS

## Task 1

**Engineering Supplies Limited invoice**

This invoice is valid for VAT purposes. It should be processed as a March input and the VAT should be reclaimed in the quarter ending March 2004.

**Alpha Stationery invoice**

This is a valid less detailed VAT invoice. It should be processed as a March input and the VAT should be reclaimed in the quarter ending March 2004.

**Jamieson & Co invoice**

This is a proforma invoice. As such it cannot be regarded as an input until a valid invoice is received. The VAT should not be reclaimed until a valid VAT invoice is received.

# Task 2

## Value Added Tax Return

For the period
01 01 01 to 31 03 01

For Official Use

Registration number: 578 4060 19

Period: 03 04

You could be liable to a financial penalty if your completed return and all the VAT payable are not received by the due date.

Due date: 30 04 01

For Official Use

081 578 4060 19 100 03 98 Q35192
MR SHERRY TEDDINGHAM
HODDLE LIMITED
22 FORMGUARD STREET
PEXLEY
PY6 3QW
219921/10

If you have a general enquiry or need advice please call our National Advice Service on 0845 010 9000

**ATTENTION**

If this return and any tax due are not received by the due date you may be liable to a surcharge.

If you make supplies of goods to another EC Member State you are required to complete an EC Sales List (VAT 101).

Before you fill in this form please read the notes on the back and the VAT Leaflet *"Filling in your VAT return"*. Fill in all boxes clearly in ink, and write 'none' where necessary. Don't put a dash or leave any box blank. If there are no pence write "00" in the pence column. Do not enter more than one amount in any box.

For official use

| | Box | £ | p |
|---|---|---|---|
| VAT due in this period on sales and other outputs | 1 | 7,740 | 12 |
| VAT due in this period on acquisitions from other EC Member States | 2 | NONE | |
| Total VAT due (the sum of boxes 1 and 2) | 3 | 7,740 | 12 |
| VAT reclaimed in this period on purchases and other inputs (including acquisitions from the EC) | 4 | 13,477 | 96 |
| **Net VAT to be paid to Customs or reclaimed by you (Difference between boxes 3 and 4)** | 5 | (5,737 | 84) |
| Total value of sales and all other outputs excluding any VAT. Include your box 8 figure | 6 | 120,606 | 00 |
| Total value of purchases and all other inputs excluding any VAT. Include your box 9 figure | 7 | 80,727 | 00 |
| Total value of all supplies of goods and related services, excluding any VAT, to other EC Member States | 8 | 10,870 | 00 |
| Total value of all acquisitions of goods and related services, excluding any VAT, from other EC Member States | 9 | NONE | 00 |

If you are enclosing a payment please tick this box. ✓

DECLARATION: You, or someone on your behalf, must sign below.

I, SHERRY TEDDINGHAM declare that the
(Full name of signatory in BLOCK LETTERS)
information given above is true and complete.

Signature .................... Date 9 April 2001

**A false declaration can result in prosecution.**

**Task 3**

## HODDLE LIMITED

22 Formguard Street, Pexley PY6 3QW
Telephone 01682 431 4322569

April 2004

HM Customs & Excise
Brendon House
14 Abbey Street
Pexley PY2 3WR

Dear Sirs

**Registration number: 578 4060 19**

The company at present accounts for VAT on a quarterly basis. We are considering the idea of changing to the cash accounting scheme, and I would be grateful if you could provide some information on this. Perhaps there is a VAT leaflet setting out details of the scheme?

The particular points for which we require further information are:

What turnover limits apply to the scheme? Are these limits affected by the fact that this company is part of a group consisting of the company itself and its parent company?

How are bad debts accounted for under the cash accounting scheme?

I would be grateful for any information you are able to provide on these points and generally about how the scheme works.

Yours faithfully

Sherry Teddingham
ACCOUNTANT

Registered office: 22 Formguard Street, Pexley PY6 3QW
Registered in England, number 2314561

**Task 4**

**CONSOLIDATED PROFIT AND LOSS ACCOUNT**
**FOR THE THREE MONTHS ENDED 31 MARCH 2004**

| | *Kelly* | *Hoddle* | *Adjustments* | *Consolidated* |
|---|---|---|---|---|
| | £ | £ | £ | £ |
| Sales | 295,768 | 120,607 | 20,167 | 396,208 |
| Opening stock | 28,341 | 14,638 | | 42,979 |
| Purchases | 136,095 | 50,908 | 18,271 | 168,732 |
| | 164,436 | 65,546 | | 211,711 |
| Closing stock | 31,207 | 16,052 | 1,896 | 49,155 |
| Cost of sales | 133,229 | *49,494 | 20,167 | 162,556 |
| Gross profit | 162,539 | 71,113 | | 233,652 |
| Wages and salaries | 47,918 | 18,014 | | 65,932 |
| Distribution expenses | 28,341 | 13,212 | | 41,553 |
| Administration expenses | 30,189 | 11,676 | | 41,865 |
| Stationery | 2,541 | *544 | | 3,085 |
| Travel | 2,001 | 267 | | 2,268 |
| Office expenses | 3,908 | 737 | | 4,645 |
| Interest payable | 12,017 | | | 12,017 |
| Other expenses | 11,765 | 3,384 | | 15,149 |
| | 138,680 | 47,834 | | 186,514 |
| Net profit for the period | 23,859 | 23,279 | | 47,138 |

* See page 345 for workings.

**Tutorial note.** You did not have to fill in the figures on this schedule but you would probably have found it helpful to do so.

**QUARTERLY CONSOLIDATED PROFIT AND LOSS ACCOUNTS**
**FOR THE YEAR ENDED 31 MARCH 2001**

| | *1 April 2003-*<br>*30 June 2003* | *1 July 2003-*<br>*30 September 2003* | *1 October 2003-*<br>*31 December 2003* | *1 January 2004 -*<br>*31 March 2004* | *1 April 2003-*<br>*31 March 2004* |
|---|---|---|---|---|---|
| | £ | £ | £ | £ | £ |
| Sales | 325,719 | 275,230 | 306,321 | 396,208 | 1,303,478 |
| Cost of sales | 134,861 | 109,421 | 121,358 | 162,556 | 528,196 |
| Gross profit | 190,858 | 165,809 | 184,963 | 233,652 | 775,282 |
| Wages and salaries | 63,314 | 61,167 | 64,412 | 65,932 | 254,825 |
| Distribution expenses | 34,217 | 30,135 | 31,221 | 41,553 | 137,126 |
| Administration expenses | 34,765 | 33,012 | 36,415 | 41,865 | 146,057 |
| Stationery | 2,981 | 2,671 | 3,008 | 3,085 | 11,745 |
| Travel | 1,975 | 1,876 | 2,413 | 2,268 | 8,532 |
| Office expenses | 4,412 | 4,713 | 3,083 | 4,645 | 16,853 |
| Interest payable | 12,913 | 12,714 | 12,432 | 12,017 | 50,076 |
| Other expenses | 10,981 | 16,421 | 15,431 | 15,149 | 57,982 |
| | 165,558 | 162,709 | 168,415 | 186,514 | 683,196 |
| Net profit for the period | 25,300 | 3,100 | 16,548 | 47,138 | 92,086 |

**Task 5**

# REPORT

**To:** Sherry Teddingham
**From:** Sol Bellcamp
**Subject:** Report on group results for the year ended 31 March 2004
**Date:** 9 April 2004

**Introduction**

This report contains the usual information on group results for the year, plus the additional information requested in your memo to me of 2 April 2004.

**Key ratios**

Gross profit margin = £775,282/£1,303,478 = 59.5%
Net profit margin = £92,086/£1,303,478 = 7.1%
Return on shareholders' capital employed = £92,086/£1,034,708 = 8.9%

**Sales revenue by quarter**

| *Quarter* | *Actual* | *Indexed (base period = first quarter 2002/03)* |
|---|---|---|
| | £ | £ |
| Apr – Jun 2003 | 325,719 | 315,511 |
| Jul – Sep 2003 | 275,230 | 264,175 |
| Oct – Dec 2003 | 306,321 | 291,005 |
| Jan – Mar 2004 | 396,208 | 379,822 |

Pie chart showing sales by quarter

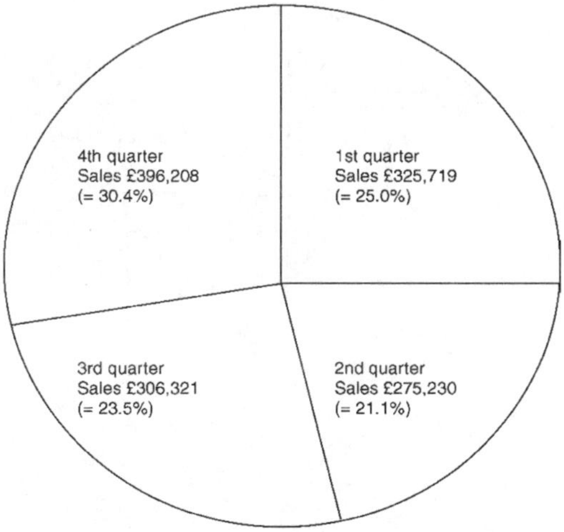

**Task 6**

**INTERFIRM COMPARISON DATA (extracts)**

Name of company ..Kelly Limited and subsidiary...............

Year ended ...31 March 2004....................................

**Data**

| | £ | *% of sales* | *Industry best* | *Industry average* |
|---|---|---|---|---|
| Sales | 1,303,478 | | | |
| Gross profit | 775,282 | 59.5% | 62.1% | 57.3% |
| Net profit | 92,086 | 7.1% | 10.4% | 5.8% |
| Fixed assets | 1,229,348 | | | |
| Current assets | 325,703 | | | |
| Current liabilities | 148,271 | | | |
| Return on capital employed | | 10.1% | 10.3% | 9.0% |

## Task 7

# MEMO

**To:** Sherry Teddingham
**From:** Sol Bellcamp
**Subject:** Interfirm comparison data
**Date:** 9 April 2004

I enclose the completed interfirm comparison data for the year ended 31 March 2004. Please let me know if you disagree with anything in it; otherwise, it is ready for despatch subject to your authorisation.

### Workings

**Task 2**

| | | £ |
|---|---|---|
| Box 4 | PDB | 12,690.53 |
| | Petty cash | 244.95 |
| | Bad debt | 73.50 |
| | Engineering Supplies invoice | 466.77 |
| | Alpha Stationery invoice | 2.21 |
| | | 13,477.96 |
| Box 7 | PDB | 79,179.67 |
| | Petty cash | 1,535.34 |
| | Alpha Stationery invoice | 12.63 |
| | | 80,727.64 |

**Task 4**

Hoddle's cost of sales, January – March 2004

| | £ |
|---|---|
| Opening stock | 14,638.00 |
| Purchases | 50,908.21 |
| | 65,546.21 |
| Closing stock | 16,052.00 |
| Cost of sales | 49,494.21 |

Hoddle's stationery costs, January – March 2004

| | £ |
|---|---|
| Petty cash book | 531.55 |
| Alpha Stationery invoice | 12.63 |
| | 544.18 |

# ORDER FORM

To: BPP Professional Education, Aldine House, Aldine Place, London, W12 8AW

Mr/Mrs/Ms (name): ______________________________

Daytime delivery address: ______________________________

Postcode: ____________ Daytime Tel No: ______________________

Please send me the following books

| | | Course Companion | Revision Companion | Combined Companion |
|---|---|---|---|---|
| **Foundation Units 1-4** | | | | |
| Units 1-4 | | ☐ £21.95 | ☐ £13.95 | |
| Office Skills (Units 21, 22, 23) | | | | ☐ £16.95 |
| **Intermediate** | | | | |
| Unit 5 | Financial Records and Accounts | ☐ £14.95 | ☐ £11.95 | |
| Units 6&7 | Cost Information and Reports and Returns | ☐ £16.95 | ☐ £12.95 | |
| **Technician** | | | | |
| Units 8&9 | Managing Performance and Controlling Resources | ☐ £15.95 | ☐ £12.95 | |
| Unit 10 | Managing Accounting Systems and People | | | ☐ £16.95 |
| Unit 11 | Drafting Financial Statements | ☐ £15.95 | ☐ £12.95 | |
| **Available November 2004** | | | | |
| Unit 15 | Cash Management and Control | | | ☐ £16.95 |
| Unit 17 | Implementing Auditing Procedures | ☐ £15.95 | ☐ £12.95 | |
| Unit 18 | Business Taxation | | | ☐ £16.95 |
| Unit 19 | Personal Taxation | | | ☐ £16.95 |
| | **Postage** | ☐ £3.00 per book | ☐ £3.00 per book | ☐ £3.00 per book |

**(Postage is charged at £3 per book to a maximum of £12)**

**Total** (inc, Postage) **£** ________

**I enclose a cheque for** ____________

or

**Please charge my Mastercard / Visa**

Card number ☐☐☐☐☐☐☐☐☐☐☐☐☐☐☐☐

Expiry Date ____________________ Start Date ____________________

Issue Number (Switch Only) ______________________________